The Organic Yenta

Maureen Goldsmith

The
Organic
Yenta

Atheneum   New York

1972

I wasn't planning on having a dedication in my book, because I always thought when I would come across them in books that they were out of place. I always got this weak feeling in my stomach whenever I read one because I felt as though I were intruding into someone's personal life. However, after writing this book and seeing what all my friends had to put up with from me, I realized just what it is for. It is to say thanks. I say thanks to everyone for putting up with all my neurotic fits and demands while putting this book together. A special thanks to all of you for still being my friends, too.

THANKS TO

Mark, Eldon, Sandee, Chuck, Sharron, Anne, Bob, Roger,
Arnelle, Bob, Judy, Ethel, Pamm, Marion, Maggie,
Jill, Jim, Roberta, the twins, Sherman
Superstar, Frank, Pierre, Bob,
Scottie, Aunt Rose, Maureen
(no relation), Marlene,
Sister Virginia,
and the boys
and girls
in the
chorus.

Contents

Who Is the Organic Yenta?

About two years ago my friend Eldon, a fast-talking advertising man (with a good soul), called me "the organic *yenta*." And it's one of those rare nicknames that really works. Organic means, to me, pure of substance, and *yenta*—well, a *yenta* is a woman who likes to stick her nose in everybody's business. Although I hate admitting it, this does describe me.

To the outside world I am a twenty-five-year-old hippie-type young woman of Jewish ancestry (healthy Russian stock), whose zest for eating good food is surpassed only by her zest for serving good food.

Unfortunately, I live alone, and except for my cats I had no one to cook for until last year, when I formed the Organic Yenta Eating Club. Now I have from twenty to thirty people at my house to cook for and eat with. They're mostly friends who either can't or won't cook but love to eat, and they pay me to concoct wonderful meals for them. Word has spread, and over the past year more and more interested patrons come every week, and whenever enough of them need a good food fix, I collect money and prepare a fine banquet, and that really does them in. Surrounded by such a large group of friends, I have risen to new heights in both organic cooking and *yenta*-ship.

When I first started cooking, my specialties were show-off things like beef Stroganoff, chicken cacciatore, shrimp creole, and other "continental" dishes, none of which were Jewish. I was going through my rebellious period; I had just left home and my identity was focused as far away from my family background as possible. But years have passed, and I have changed in many ways. The biggest change is my move over to being a "vegetarian" and concentrating on natural foods.

I think it is important to note that I have not made this change because of any new spiritual or religious commitment (although I have some compassion for those people who feel that killing animals in order for mankind to maintain itself is unnecessary and barbaric).

The main reason I became interested in natural foods was to please a man I was dating, who has since jilted me. When he became a vegetarian I had to learn how to cook for him in order to keep him captivated. As I became more and more involved, I began to be interested in the food itself and also in the people who shopped in the natural food stores. They all looked so healthy and happy; I was sure it was the right road to be on. Besides, my enjoyment of shopping was greater because of all the gorgeous men who shop at natural food stores; my glands really get a workout whenever I go to fill my pantry. The smell is wonderful, too. It is interesting that when you enter a big supermarket you smell exactly what you are buying: chemicals and more chemicals. In the natural food stores you smell nature.

Although my first vegetarian man has since gone, my interest in healthy cooking remains. And I have learned that whatever value meat may have for me can be obtained in a more appealing way than by killing animals. When you stop to think about it, you may find you actually never liked meat very much. I know I never did. But, traditionally, meat is forced down our throats as a necessity. And we are always told how delicious a thick steak or a juicy roast is. But ever since I can remember, I have hated meat and always had to smother it with catsup to tolerate it at all. As a child, I didn't know why, but if a hamburger wasn't on a big bun with mounds of onions, relish, and catsup, it wasn't any good. Finally

I realized I'd be just as happy with the bread, onions, relish, and catsup. Later, when I grew up, if I served beef Stroganoff at a party, I would get off on the sauce over the noodles and just forget the meat.

This is how I progressed to where I am now. I have to admit that I still get a craving for cold cuts, but that's because of the spices in them.

I do like fish, though, and I still eat it occasionally. But my favorites are shrimp, lobster, crab meat, etc., which are considered *traif* (not to be eaten by Jews). I will therefore devote a special chapter, entitled "Traif," to these forbidden foods.

I found that along with my change to natural foods has come a rebirth in my interest in Jewish cooking. In Jewish cooking there is already a split between meat meals and nonmeat meals—*fleishig* and *milchig*. I began to go back over my life to remember *milchig* meals we used to have when I was a little girl. I wanted to turn my friends on to my "new" Jewish dishes, because most of my friends are *goyim* (non-Jews) and hadn't tasted any of the foods I had grown up with and taken for granted, so I slowly began slipping these dishes into the regular menus for my eating club. The response was quite exciting.

I had originally strayed from the strict Jewish menus because I wasn't satisfied with the blandness of many of the meals. There was no emphasis on a variety of spices, so there was no excitement. All you could count on was that you would walk away full—if you could still walk. For the most part "health foods," too, suffer from blandness, but in addition many of them leave you starving. So I put health foods and Jewish foods together and added my own touch of splendor: I like spicy foods, and that is how I cook— natural and spicy!

So I went further than the Jewish dishes and adapted any recipe I could to organic foods. And what a surprise . . . It's a wonder when I stop and think that I am actually doing myself good while I am totally enjoying myself.

All my friends who eat at the Organic Yenta always ask for

ingredients and recipes. This book presents them and you with the most complete collection of Organic Yenta recipes ever gathered in one place. I had to search through two apartments in San Francisco and one in Chicago to get it together. But before you get into it, let me give you a few warnings.

I rarely if ever put in any ingredients that I don't personally like —for instance, raisins and all other dried fruit. I hate them—I really do. So I never use any of them in my cooking, no matter who it's for. However, I will write in "optional ingredients" for many of my recipes.

I think it is also good to mention that I don't believe there is such a thing as a definite recipe—there is only a suggested basic combination of ingredients. I never make something the same way twice. One day I may be in the mood for more or less of a certain herb or spice than I was the day before—or maybe I'm completely out of an ingredient. So I don't think you should follow a recipe exactly in hopes of being a good cook. I think a good cook is someone who knows what she likes and what tastes good to her * and works from that. I rarely use any measuring spoons except when I'm trying a recipe for the first time. I just trust my taste, and I think you should do the same thing. I call myself "a pincher and a pourer." What I've done in writing this book is to measure my pinches and pours in order to make it easier for you.

I'm sure you'll like the recipes.

---

* I would write "he," because I know that's what you are supposed to do if you mean a person in general. But I'd like to score a point for Women's Lib.

I

Before You
Start to Cook

Your Kitchen

Kitchen Utensils

The following items are what I consider to be essential for me in the kitchen. I function perfectly if I have just these things available. Unfortunately, I often lend things to my friends, and whenever I go to use something there is a possibility of its not being there. I always manage to make do, so what I'm trying to tell you is that, if you don't have all these things at your disposal, go ahead anyway. I'm sure that you can make do, too.

Blender. To me there is no substitute for a blender. Either you have one or you don't. I don't, so a friend of mine who doesn't use his very much has lent me his. To me they are really indispensable, and once you have one you will find hundreds of uses for it aside from the suggested uses that come with it. If you are in the market for one, why not watch the papers for a sale at your local discount or department store so that you can save a little money and maybe get a really good one?

Bowls. I use the same bowls for mixing as I do for serving salads and cooked vegetables. I just have a group of different bowls that I collect in different ways. I get some at garage sales and some at secondhand stores, and some I just buy in regular stores because I like them. The more you have, the better. I find that I never have enough bowls. However, I don't have enough space for them either, and that can create a problem.

Bread board. This is very useful for kneading bread and for rolling out any kind of dough. Bread can be kneaded or rolled out on any surface, but I prefer the board because it can be transported anywhere, and somehow it seems to me that I make less of a mess with the board than I did when I was using my table top. I waited a long time before I got mine because I didn't know where I was going to put it. The solution was to just drill a hole in the top and hang it on the wall with a cup hook.

Canner. The one that I use is easily obtainable; I got it at an army surplus store. It is the kind that is dark blue porcelain, with white speckles in it, and it has a removable rack in it for setting jars in. This is what I use for making my yogurt. When you take the rack out you have a big pot that is great for making a jumbo batch of spaghetti sauce if you are having a big party.

Chopping board. This is necessary to prevent you from cutting up your table tops and counters.

Colander. This is essential for rinsing off vegetables and straining cooked noodles and macaroni.

Cookie sheet. I find that at least one cookie sheet is a kitchen necessity; and even though it costs more, I recommend that yours be stainless steel.

Double boiler. I use my double boiler for making lots of different sauces; and you can always take it apart to have two separate saucepans.

Flame trivet. This item I find to be a real gem. It sits on top of the flame itself, and then you put your pot or skillet on top of it. It prevents anything from ever sticking and controls the flame for you while cooking your food carefully. Another name for it is "flame tamer," and I suggest that you be sure and get one that has an asbestos handle cover, because they do get very hot. Here is a hint: My friend Sandee, who also uses one all the time, says that she doesn't need a double boiler because of the flame trivet. She says that she can control the flame well enough with the trivet to get the results she needs from the double boiler.

Flour sifter. When I was a little girl the most horrible thing about baking was having to sift the dry ingredients. Then they invented presifted flour, and I thought that it was a gift from heaven just for me. Well, I threw my mother's sifter away, and I thought that I was oh so modern. Ha, I spent a whole day at the flea market looking for a flour sifter one Sunday because I am now back to the old method. There is no such thing as presifted flour at the health food store where I shop. They mill the flour fresh every day, and when you use it you have to sift it. (Whole-grain flours that you buy at the health food stores hopefully are much fresher than those you can get at the supermarkets, and they do contain much more of the nutrients because they haven't been milled out and used for other purposes, as is done with the commercial supermarket flours. Thus whole-grain flours may be more work, but I think they are worth it.)

Funnel. It is even a good idea to have a few different-size funnels for the different-size jars that you may be pouring liquids into. You can buy plastic ones, which I consider to be more desirable than aluminum.

Glass baking dishes. I use glass in all my baking. It is easy, cleans well, and there is no danger with it at all. Just remember one thing: Most recipes are geared for aluminum pans, and glass cooks faster than aluminum. Thus you should always lower the temperature of your oven 25 degrees when you cook with a glass dish.

Glass jars. Easily accessible; all you do is save the jars you buy at the store when you empty them. I don't bother with anything smaller than one quart. I also went to a glass factory and bought some one-gallon jars. I store all my dry goods from the store in various-size jars with tight lids. This keeps everything fresh, and also protects them from any little crawling visitors that may be lurking in the walls and pipes. I also use the jars for canning purposes and of course for making my yogurt.

Grater. I hate grating! It seems that I always lose a bit of skin no matter what precautions I take. It does help when you are making cheese sauces or cole slaw, though.

Hand mixer. I don't have a big electric mixer, so I make all my cakes and batters that need fast mixing with this. I'm satisfied that it is enough.

Juicer. I have this old juice squeezer that I got in a junk store for fifty cents. I put the orange or lemon on top of the cup and then push down on the handle. Presto, fresh-squeezed juice. It is good only for oranges, lemons, and small grapefruits, but that is all I need now. Other fruits can be put into the blender and whizzed around to get the juice out, and then strained if you want.

Knives. I always manage to ruin every knife I get. However, it is important to have at least two good paring knives (one to use and the other one to use when you have misplaced the first one), one bread knife, and one or more sharp chopping knives for vegetables. (I often misplace the chopping knives, too.)

Measuring spoons. A good idea is to hang them on the wall some place where they are easily accessible. I have two sets of measuring spoons, too, because I have a habit of throwing them in the sink, which can become very crowded very fast, and then needing them again and being unable to find them. Thus, with two sets I have a good chance of finding a clean one in a pinch.

Measuring cups. The same goes with measuring cups. I have two 1-cup measurers, one 2-cup measurer, and one 4-cup measurer. There always is at least one clean when I need it.

Mortar and pestle. I can honestly say that this is one of my most indispensable kitchen accessories. I use it to crush my sea salt down to a soft and functional consistency, and to crush garlic and small amounts of nuts and seeds. It also crushes cloves and peppercorns. I really dig mine and enjoy using it. They aren't too expensive, and they are made out of various materials. Mine is wood.

Peeler. When I was growing up my mother called it a "potato peeler" or a "carrot peeler." I just call it "the peeler," because I use it on beets, eggplant, cucumber (sometimes), tomatoes (sometimes), and various other vegetables, not to mention fruits like peaches, nectarines, pears, and plums.

Pepper mill. I can't begin to emphasize the difference fresh-ground pepper makes on food. I use it all the time. The pepper mill, however, doesn't give you too much at one time, so it is mostly for use on salads and already prepared foods that need "just a hint."

Pots and pans. It is my belief that stainless steel is the best for use in cooking food. Unfortunately, I have not been able to afford a complete set of stainless steel yet, so I have a set of porcelain-coated iron cookware that I use. I like them very much, and there is no danger in using them. I find it necessary to have at least three saucepans. I have 1-quart, 2-quart, and 3-quart saucepans, none of which go unused. I also have a Dutch oven, which is stainless steel and the most valuable piece of cookware that I have because it doubles as a vegetable steamer for me. Skillets are important because you need them for sautéing vegetables. I also use them for various sauce-based dishes and for the little frying that I do, but mostly I value them for sautéing. Be sure to include a large one for when you are sautéing a large quantity of vegetables for a certain dish—mushrooms, for instance.

Pot holders. How often do you burn yourself in the kitchen? Well, I have no solution for you, because I burn myself at least that much. I have one little hint, and that is to put a pot holder on top of anything that you are cooking that has a lid on it. That way, whenever you go to test it you will be reminded by the presence of the pot holder that the pan is hot and you should be cautious. Have lots of pot holders around if you are the type who misplaces them a lot. I'm like that, and if I don't have a lot of them all over the kitchen I get lazy and then oops, another burn. They are easy to make and make nice gifts, too, if you resent having to buy them. I use different colors of felt and make patchwork or collage pot holders, which don't cost me too much and are entertaining for me to do.

Rolling pin. I have a nice wooden rolling pin. I also have some little stockings that I bought (I think they were about a dollar for three, and they are washable), and I put them over the pin to prevent the dough from sticking to the pin. One thing I acquired at a junk store that is really worth telling about is an old glass rolling pin. It is hollow with a screw top at one end. What you do is fill the pin with water and then refrigerate it until the water is good and cold (overnight is good), and then roll out your dough. It is especially good for pie crust, which to be honest is all I have ever used it for.

Rubber spatula. Good for scraping bowls, and for when you have measured a heavy liquid like honey and have to pour it into whatever you are making. It enables you to get the entire amount out and thus retain accuracy.

Salt grinder. Not essential, but I find mine very useful. After I grind my sea salt up in the mortar and pestle I put some of it into the salt grinder, which grinds it a little finer for when I need a little salt on a salad or a vegetable or in soup.

Spice rack. I find it necessary to have *all* my spices easily available. Although I have a very cute spice rack made of nice oak, it wasn't big enough for all the things that I find necessary to have around. So, I had my friend Pierre nail an orange crate up on a wall in the kitchen to hold all my different spices and cooking additions. Everything is at eye level, and this is helpful in maintaining good organization.

Steamer. A good vegetable steamer is very expensive, and thus I haven't been able to buy one as yet. There are different types of baskets and stands that can be placed in a deep pan and used to steam vegetables. I use a vegetable basket with handles, which I place over the sides of my Dutch oven when I put the basket into it. I put just enough water into the bottom of the pan to create steam but not touch any of the vegetables, and then cover the pan with the lid, thus holding the basket in place. Believe it or not, this method works fine, and I am totally satisfied with my steamed vegetables.

Strainer. I find it helpful to have more than one of these, too. I have two, of different sizes—one for big jobs like sauces and juices and one for little jobs like teas.

Trivets. I use mosaic tiles that I pick up here and there to put hot casserole dishes and pans on, for cooling and for serving. They are quite functional and add a little color to my kitchen. A nice thing to do is to cut a piece of felt to cover the back of the tile to prevent any scratching of wood surfaces or counter tops. It glues on easily with a little Elmer's Glue, or whatever you prefer.

Vegetable brush. For scrubbing vegetables clean before using them in your cooking. If you don't want to use a brush, just rub the vegetables well under running water until they are very clean and smooth.

Wire whisk. The whisk is very helpful in whipping and in blending liquids together. It took me a while to get used to using one, but now I really value mine. If you are buying one for the first time, be careful, because there are some that are made poorly: these are the ones that are made of all wire, including the handle. The wooden-handled one that I have is over a year old and it is in fine shape; I doubt if it will ever fall apart.

Wok. This is the most essential cooking utensil in a Chinese kitchen. Although I do not have a Chinese kitchen, I am very attached to my wok. You can use it to sauté and fry without unnecessary use of fat. Vegetables can be cooked in small amounts of oil quickly and thus retain their crispness and fresh color and, most important, their vitamins and minerals.

Wooden spoons. I have gotten to the point over the past two years where I don't use anything but wood for all my cooking, serving, and mixing. Wooden spoons have a great value to a good cook. They prevent scratching on the surface of your pots and pans; they don't puncture or damage by bruising any of the vegetables that you may be cooking; and they don't conduct heat if you happen to leave them in a pan in which you are cooking something, so if you go back and touch the spoon you don't get burned. However, there is one problem. Be careful, if you lay them down on the stove, that you don't set them too close to a flame—I've lost quite a few that way. The wood smells good when it burns, but what a waste!

There Is a System to Setting Up a Kitchen

Over the past five years I have lived in as many as six different places, and as I left each one I learned a little more about setting up a household, especially the kitchen. I have been at my current address for almost two years, and I believe that I have finally mastered the art of making my kitchen function for me. I can only speak from my own experience and from my own observation of my friends, but I definitely think that the first important rule in setting up a kitchen is: Take full advantage of all the space available to you and make it work for you. I think that everything should have a certain place where it belongs, and if it can be in sight, then that is all the better for you. I screw cup hooks into all the available molding space and hang everything in a certain spot. That way everything is in view, and handy whenever I need it. My spices are all arranged in the orange crate that I had my friend Pierre nail up on the wall. The orange crate being there creates more storage space, because the top of it became a shelf on which I was able to place a jar of cereal, my mortar and pestle, and a plant. (I think that every kitchen should have plants, but they should not get in the way of work or storage space. That is why most of the plants that I have in my kitchen are hanging from the ceiling.)

Near my sink there was a small wall that was doing nothing, and I felt the need to put it to work. I had Pierre nail another fruit crate up, and thus I was able to store all my cleaning needs and again acquire another shelf, on which I was able to store my big honey can and a couple more glass jars containing different things at different times.

The more tiny walls the better. As long as you aren't endangered by the addition of boxes or shelves on the walls, then I say fill them up. Make everything as easily accessible as possible, and I am sure that your kitchen will become a room of fun and enjoyment instead of a room of chore.

Now, if you have a small amount of wall space somewhere and a box won't fit and, say, a shelf would be dangerous, then put some cup hooks up and hang different things that have handles or holes in them—for example, the flour sifter, the strainers, the measuring cups, the colander, and maybe even your pots and pans. Try and put things back in the same place again and again after use, and soon you will have a system all your own in which everything will just flow into your hands.

I find that at least one good counter area is necessary in the kitchen. My kitchen is so small that I can't even fit a table and chairs into it. I was able, however, to get a small old table into a corner, and I use it as my work area. On top of it I keep my blender, nut grinder, chopping block, juice squeezer, and a plant. It is a bit crowded, but it is the best that I can do. Whenever I have work to do I just sort of push things to the side and make do. It is good, though, because everything is at least in a convenient spot. I roll out my dough here, too, so things aren't too bad.

There are, however, people with kitchens even smaller than mine. Take my sister Pamm, for instance. Her kitchen was so small there was barely any room for the sink, stove, and refrigerator. There was, though, about three feet between the end of her stove and the back door, so I decided that the only solution was to get a piece of wood and do some cutting into it and nail some legs to it and squeeze it into that little space. Well, it worked, and now she has a decent counter top where she can at least chop a few vegetables and mix a few batters. We also managed to get a piece of wood cut small enough to fit into a tiny space above the counter and we put that up as a shelf for her spices. The shelf being up left a vacant space between the counter and the shelf, so we screwed in some cup hooks and up went her measuring spoons and a few other odds and ends.

Go in and take a good look around. I am sure that you will find a lot of small areas that can be converted into working space. I have a window that doesn't open and is to me useless. However, that window has a windowsill and that windowsill is now stacked with glass jars, whose lids have been painted happy colors, full of different nuts, seeds, beans, and noodles. I must say it looks nice, and I am relieved from the lack of storage space.

Many people have pantries, and I think that is nice, but for the most part I think people abuse the use of a pantry. I don't think that anyone should have any more food in her house than she needs for a few days' meals. Foods should be bought fresh and eaten fresh. I believe that the original use for a pantry was to store foods that were put up in the summer and in the fall, like relishes, pickles, jellies, etc., but that it somehow became a collection spot for foods that just get stale and useless as far as food value goes. I try to go to the store at least three times a week. I don't enjoy it, but I do believe it to be beneficial, and what is more important? Thus if you do have a pantry, I suggest that you either get into canning or use it for storing some of your kitchenware that you don't have any other place for.

Another handy hint that I have for you is to put all your wooden spoons (or whatever you use for stirring, mixing, and blending) in a container on top of your stove. Thus they are always there for you.

Shopping Guide

Know Your Health Food Store

Unfortunately, I haven't been able to check out all the different health food stores throughout the country. The only ones that I really do know are the ones here in San Francisco, although I have been through a few in Chicago and in New York. Many of the products are the same, only the prices vary from coast to coast. I am convinced that almost everything you might want can be obtained in a pure form from a health food store. If the one near you doesn't carry organic spices, for instance, it is probably because they don't have a big enough demand for them. I didn't see them in any of the health food stores in Chicago or New York, but I did see them in a tiny roadside health food store in Connecticut. So they do exist. The best thing to do is to get to know your organic merchant and not to be afraid to ask him any questions that you may have on your mind. That was a big problem with me. I didn't know enough about organic foods and I was afraid to ask. I try hard now not to be shy and ask questions a lot.

Some stores can't carry certain products because of health laws, and you should know about this, too. Take yogurt, for instance. There is a culture in the yogurt called "acidophilus bacteria," which is also termed "friendly bacteria" because it aids in the digestion process of your intestines. In Chicago there is some silly law that states that pure yogurt cannot be sold in licensed stores, so it is not available—although it is in a suburb of Chicago.

Some health food stores can be a hoax, too, and it is up to you to be able to determine this. If you find that all their grains, seeds, and flours are prepackaged at the factory, I would be a little wary. I have read that whole grains and nuts are likely to loose a lot of their nutritional value within ten days after they have been milled. So if you are buying grains that have already been milled before they even reached the store, I would question their value. At the store where I shop they have their own mill, as do many stores in this area, and they process their grains and nuts fresh every day. They don't put out more than they think they need, and if they are out of something, you can either wait for them to grind it or come back another day. This may seem inconvenient, but at least it is a guarantee of freshness and dependability.

Even though you may be in a health food store, that doesn't mean that you shouldn't read the labels on the things that you are about to buy. I do trust the store that I shop in, but that trust has been arrived at after checking out over ten different stores in the area.

If you are buying your dairy products in the health food store, be careful to note their freshness. They don't for the most part use the pasteurization process on the dairy products sold in the health food stores here in San Francisco, so they must always be purchased fresh and used within a day or two or else they will become rancid. I must honestly say that I purchase most of my dairy products at the regular supermarket. Only those cheeses that have been processed or that have dyes in them are to my belief really dangerous.

One fact that is important to keep in mind is that, if you are shopping in an honest health food store, all the foods sold there will be completely free of unnatural preservatives. I say "unnatural," because many things have lecithin in them and lecithin works as a natural preservative to some degree. However, this isn't enough to allow anyone to indulge in overshopping. The fact that most foods have no preservatives in them doesn't make them bad for you, it makes them good for you. Those preservatives are almost all chemicals that are not digestible and can do nothing but serious damage to your intestines, kidneys, and liver. The point that I am trying to make is that you should buy only what you need: *no more than that*. The same applies to fruits and vegetables. The ones that are sold as organic in the store have not been sprayed or injected, so they are going to spoil sooner. This will do you no harm if you haven't bought any more than you need. This whole system is very appealing to me, because, if somehow we can learn not to grow more than we need, then maybe we can help our lands to last longer by not overusing them.

Because there are no preservatives, almost everything that you buy in a health food store that comes in a package or container does need refrigeration. That is also why nothing can be purchased in a jumbo "family size" package. I suggest, too, that everything you can buy in bulk, like grains, rice, nuts, noodles, beans, etc., still be bought in moderation. Try shopping once a week for these items and be sure that you put each of them in some kind of an airtight container as soon as possible to preserve their freshness. Again, I must emphasize: Do not overshop.

There Still Is a Use for the Supermarket

The most important thing to always remember to do is to read the ingredients of everything you are considering purchasing. You and no one else are your own guide as to just what is going to go into your body. There is no reason for me to go up and down the aisles of a grocery store with you and tell you what I avoid and why. The answer is—almost everything. However, there are still some things that I do go to a supermarket for, and I will talk about them. First and foremost are the dairy products. I buy cottage cheese, sour cream, cream cheese, butter (I never use margarine because it is synthetic), milk, and most cheeses that have not been processed and that definitely do not have any dyes in them. The main reason I do this is because the cost of dairy products at the supermarket is much less. I know that I should buy them at the health food store, but everyone has his certain weak spot, and this is mine. I really don't think that I am doing myself too much harm, because dairy products for the most part are pretty pure, and hopefully the animals that these products come from are fed on good grains.

I also purchase there vegetables and fruits that are considered tropical because they can't be grown in this country, and so there is no way of telling how they have been grown. I am referring to bananas and pineapples and certain types of figs. The health food stores carry them and say that to their knowledge they aren't organic, so I just buy them at the supermarket because they are cheaper there.

In many of the big chain-store operations across the country there is a trend toward including a small organic foods section. If you come across one be sure and check it out, because you may find that they are carrying some of the same things as your favorite health food store at a much cheaper price. For instance, there is a certain cereal that is made of whole oats and almonds with honey that I am very fond of. It comes in a sixteen-ounce package and sells for eighty cents at the health food store; at the supermarket that I go to I can get the same thing for fifty cents. That is a savings that warrants your investigation. Apple juice, which has become the cola of the health food stores, can also be purchased in the regular supermarket at a good saving.

Paper products must also be purchased in the supermarket. I won't say much about these because they are off the subject; however, I feel the need to inform you that the dyes that they put into paper towels, toilet paper, paper handkerchiefs, and paper napkins are not in any way bio-degradable and thus they pollute the air and our waterways. Please try using plain old white. After a while you may even learn to like the simplicity of it. It took me a while, but I have. The same holds true with the bio-degradable detergents that are available. They may not look as fancy or smell as glamorous, but they do their job without doing any damage. Don't you think that is worth changing over to them? The supermarkets here in California have all been stocking bio-degradable washing products for quite some time now, and I'm sure if your stores aren't carrying them now you can do something to influence them.

Most of the foods that are on the shelves in the supermarket's gourmet section, which are usually imported, I find to be usable in certain instances. Read the labels for ingredients and see for yourself. I buy a lot of the crackers and hard breads that are imported because they are made from whole grains and have no preservatives, and particularly because I find that they are as good as anything else that I can buy.

Some Things You Never Did Before and Why You Should Start Now

Grow Your Own Herbs and Spices

If you have a nice little house somewhere with a garden area, then you are very lucky, because you can have a very nice herb garden of your own at very little expense and even less work. However, if you are like me, living in an apartment in a city, it becomes more difficult to grow anything of your own. There is a risk in setting up a pseudo garden on the roof or on the back porch because the neighborhood cats are bound to sniff it out and claim it for themselves.

There are little kits, which can be bought in most nurseries, that allow you to start your own little herb garden in a nice sunny window. They customarily have six cups in them containing the most commonly used herbs, like orégano, basil, marjoram, tarragon, rosemary, and chives. They usually develop fairly well and then require transplanting into larger pots. You can control them for a while, though, by trimming them enough so that they don't have to be transplanted too often. You can also buy herb plants that have already been started. It is important that they have a lot of light, and it is suggested that you keep them in the kitchen so you are always aware of them and thus more likely to use them. If you pick your herbs fresh from the plant to use them, then you should always use about twice as much as you would if they were dried.

You can also buy seeds and start them yourself in well-irrigated pots in soil that you can be sure is organic. This is the system that I prefer, although it is the most difficult and often very disappointing. If you buy your herb plants already started, you can transplant them into good rich soil that you buy, which is close to organic, I think. If you don't have a wide enough windowsill, try building a shelf into one of your kitchen windows, with side brackets to hold it up. Then you can set your plants up on it and enjoy them.

In the summer, when the herbs are full and flowering, you should cut them down and dry a lot of each one and then bottle them for the coming year. Cut off only the perfect leaves; the leaves will be so plentiful that you will be able to choose. Do the cutting in the morning and then lay the leaves on a cookie sheet and put them into a slow oven (200°) and leave the door open. Watch them carefully and turn them every few minutes. When they become dry enough so that they begin to crumble, take them out of the oven and crush them with your mortar and pestle. When you like the size of the pieces, then you are done. Put them into a cute little jar that you have been saving for something special and be sure to label it.

Grow Your Own Sprouts

Seeds that can be sprouted:

Alfalfa	*Soybeans*
Mung beans	*Flax*
Lentils	

Put enough of your desired seeds in the bottom of a clean jar to cover it. Fill the jar halfway with spring water, and then place a piece of cheesecloth over the top of the jar and tighten it with a rubber band to hold it on. *No lid!* Let it sit overnight. In the morning empty the jar and rinse the seeds well. Return them to the jar and replace the cheesecloth. No water this time. Rinse them every day until they sprout to where you like them.

Sprouts are most healthful when they are only one-quarter to one-half inch long because you still have the benefit of some of the seed being left. Thus you have the sprout, which is a live food when you eat it because it still is in its growing state, and you have some of the seed, too, which is the natural state of the food. But they can be eaten when longer, which is how they come when you buy them in the store. This is how I like them best myself.

One reason sprouts are so good for you is that they are alive when you are eating them. What I mean is that they are still growing, whereas any other food, even vegetables, is not really alive when you eat it, because it has been removed from the place where it received its nutritional feeding.

Make Your Own Tomato Sauce

There are a few things that I still would buy in a can at the supermarket, if I would let myself: tomato sauce, tomato paste, and just peeled tomatoes in the can are among the few. I have managed to find a quick way to get these things together, though, so I guess I shouldn't complain too much. Tomatoes in the can that you use in cooking are just softened tomatoes that have been boiled a little and then had the skin peeled off. This you can do yourself. If you can find where the local produce center for your city is, then you should go there and buy a bunch of softened tomatoes from them. Take them home and wash them well. Then place them in some boiling water for about 10 minutes. Remove and let them cool for a few minutes and then peel them. Now you have fresh, whole peeled tomatoes (hopefully even organic), which you can use in a variety of dishes, from spaghetti sauce to Mommy's Baked Beans (page 59).

If your goal was to have tomato sauce, then cut the tomatoes up after you have peeled them and put them into your blender and whiz them around until a liquid forms. Now strain it through your strainer and then cook it over a low heat for about an hour, adding arrowroot starch a little at a time until it begins to thicken. Keep stirring it so that it doesn't lump or burn. You can also cook some onion and some spices in it, but I usually leave the spicing up till later, when I start to make whatever dish it is that I am going to make. When the sauce is thick enough, remove it from the heat.

Make Your Own Granola

Granola is a very popular breakfast cereal that has really caught on here in the past few years. I must say that there is a company in Paradise, California, that puts out a packaged granola that is pretty good, although it does need some trimmings. This company is called the Lassen Company; they also make another cereal called Honey Almond Crunch that I like so much that I have begun to use it and not make my own any more. I can't begin to tell you what a difference it is to eat whole grains and oats instead of the garbage that we grew up on. Until I discovered the Honey Almond Crunch and the granola I hadn't had any breakfast cereal in about five years. Now I eat it almost every morning with a little banana or whatever berries happen to be in season. All my friends like it with raisins, so I feel obligated to tell you that it is possible that you could, too, if you are into raisins.

GRANOLA

MAKES ABOUT 10 SERVINGS

¾ cup light vegetable oil
1 cup boiling water (spring water, if possible)
½ cup whole-wheat flour

3 ½ cups rolled oats

½ cup ground pumpkin seeds

½ cup ground sesame seeds

½ cup ground sunflower seeds

½ cup wheat germ

1 cup shredded coconut

1 tablespoon sea salt

1 cup chopped nuts

½ cup raisins (optional)

1 teaspoon vanilla extract

1 cup honey or maple sugar or date sugar (These sugars are pretty expensive, so I rarely use them)

Mix the oil with the boiling water. In a large bowl place all the dry ingredients except the chopped nuts and raisins and toss them around until they are mixed up pretty well. Then combine the vanilla extract and the honey with the boiling water and oil and pour the mixture over the dry ingredients, sort of stirring it around till the liquid is taken up by the dry ingredients. Don't let it get too wet. As soon as the liquid is distributed well enough, spread the mixture over a cookie sheet and bake it slowly at about 200° for 2 to 3 hours. Watch it carefully and check it often to make sure that it doesn't get too brown around the edges. Keep turning it about and break up any big chunks that may still be there.

When the mixture is dry enough, remove it from the oven and let it cool. Place it in the large bowl again, add the chopped nuts and the raisins, and toss. Now place the mixture evenly in jars with tight lids. (If you have the time, why not paint the lids? Then you can make a gift out of the granola.)

When you have the granola for breakfast, don't be afraid to add a little fresh fruit. You will find that you don't need too much of it to fill you up. Just a little milk or cream when you serve it, and if you want a little more honey—though I doubt that you will need it.

Make Your Own Yogurt

It took me a long time before I even was willing to taste yogurt. I didn't know exactly what it was about it, but I was very hesitant.

Then last week a friend of mine's mother said something that made me do a little reflecting. We were talking about yogurt, and she said that she hated it. I said oh, how can you say that, have you tasted it? and her reply was no! I can't even stand the word or the way it sounds. Well, I think that was something that influenced me for a long time, too. I do like it now, and eat it a lot. There is no doubt in my mind that it is one of the most healthful dairy products there is around. I am partial to plain yogurt that I can make myself and that I can add things to, as opposed to the prepared yogurt that already contains fruit and sweeteners. But no matter what kind you prefer, there is no doubt as to the fact that it is goooood for you.

YOGURT

2 quarts spring water
1½ cups powdered milk
2 tablespoons yogurt culture or plain commercial yogurt (I use Johnston's Yogurt if I don't already have some made, because it is the purest and has nothing added to it)
1 can condensed milk

Mix 2 cups spring water, the powdered milk, and the yogurt culture in the blender. Then add the condensed milk. Pour the mixture into 2 quart jars equally. Then fill the jars with spring water to about 1 inch from the rim of the jar. Stir the ingredients and then place the lids on the jars, but don't tighten them. Place the jars in a canning pan with just enough tap water in it to touch the outside of the jar level with the yogurt mixture (no more water than that).

Place the canner in a warm, but not hot, place (about 105°–120°) for 3 hours, or until the yogurt sets. (I place it inside the oven with just the pilot light on.)

When the yogurt has set, remove the jars, wipe dry, tighten lids, and refrigerate. Wait 24 hours *if you can*, and, boy, what a treat! You even have your own culture now.

I eat yogurt plain sometimes, but more often than not I doctor it up with a little something else. Here are some of the different ways that I use it.

VANILLA-HONEY YOGURT

¼ teaspoon vanilla extract   *1 cup yogurt*
1 teaspoon honey

Mix the vanilla and the honey into the yogurt and eat it. It is just about the same as eating it plain, only some of the tartness is gone.

You can also try different flavors of honey. Each will have a little different zing when added to the yogurt.

BERRY YOGURT

For every jar of yogurt that you want to add berries to, add ¾ cup of fresh, in-season berries. You can now eat it or put it back into jars. I don't add any honey when I mix in the berries, because I like to rely on the sweetness of the fruit. That doesn't mean that you can't add some honey, though. Just not too much, because then there isn't any reason for you to have added the berries.

YOGURT AND FRUIT

Cut up some apples or pears or oranges and pour some yogurt over them. There isn't any reason why you can't use all of them. Pineapple is good with yogurt when you can get it in season, cheap.

YOGURT AND DATES

Chop up about ½ cup dates and add them to 2 cups yogurt. You can add a little honey, but not too much. About ¼ cup chopped walnuts would be good here, too.

CHUCK'S SPECIAL

Now, I'm not guaranteeing that you will like this one, but I'm sure that it's worth a try. One day while I was visiting my friend Chuck, he decided that he was hungry, which is usually the case with him, so we went into the kitchen, where he proceeded to pour out a bowl of yogurt and then add about 4 big spoonfuls of fresh peanut butter. I was disgusted and did a big belch, but when I tried it I was really turned on. It is an interesting combination that should be tried at least once. My only problem is that I like it and now have trouble controlling myself, because we all know how fattening peanut butter is, don't we? Protein or no protein.

Make Your Own Mayonnaise

Mayonnaise is a sauce that to me has great value. It can be used as it is on many things, and it can be used in complementing many other sauces, spreads, and dressings. However, mayonnaise as we know it calls for the use of eggs, which many people who eat health foods leave out of their diets due to their high concentration of cholesterol. (Cholesterol from eggs is very hard to digest, and there are simpler forms that can be obtained.) Thus I am going to give two simple recipes for mayonnaise. One with eggs in it and one without.

MAYONNAISE

ABOUT 1 CUP

1 egg, at room temperature
Pinch of dry mustard
¼ teaspoon salt

1½ teaspoons lemon juice,
approximately
½ cup light vegetable oil,
approximately

Break the egg into your blender and add the dry mustard and the salt. Whiz the blender at a high speed for a few seconds at a time until the egg mixture thickens and is a bit foamy. Now add the lemon juice and whiz again for a few seconds. If you have a blender with a hole in the middle of the lid that has a top on it that you can remove, remove it. Or remove the entire top. Begin pouring the oil in a little at a time while the blender is going at a high speed. Watch it carefully and keep adding the oil very slowly until you see it begin to thicken. When you have the desired thickness, then you are done. If it doesn't develop a desirable thickness, then add a little more oil until it does. If you happen to get it too thick, then add a little more lemon juice. Never make more than you need for a few days at a time. First, because it can spoil due to the fact that it has no preservatives in it, and, second, because it is always better fresh.

ORGANIC MAYONNAISE

ABOUT 1 PINT

¾ cup spring water
½ cup cider vinegar
1½ teaspoons honey

½ teaspoon dry mustard
1 cup powdered milk
2 cups light vegetable oil

In the blender, combine all the ingredients except the oil. Then, while the blender is running at a low speed, slowly add the oil. When the desired consistency develops, stop with the oil.

Make Your Own Jiffy Jellies and Jams

I am a real nut for fresh fruit "in season." I have found a great way to have fresh fruit in a jelly-type consistency that makes a wonderful treat with freshly baked bread. It is also good on older bread or crackers for breakfast or at lunch.

To begin with, you can use practically any fruit or berry that you happen to have around. (I usually only use one fruit at a time, but there is no reason why you can't use different combinations if you happen to have a variety around.)

MAKES A LITTLE MORE THAN A CUP

Strawberries	*Apricots (must be soft)*
Blueberries	*Nectarines (must be soft)*
Blackberries	*Pears (must be soft)*
Peaches (must be soft)	*Raspberries*
Plums (must be soft)	

Okay, these are just some of the fruits that I have used. Anyway, cut the fruit up into little pieces, about 1½ cups. If you use berries, just slice them once or twice. Make a mixture of ½ cup honey, ½ cup spring water, and 2 teaspoons arrowroot starch. Pour it into a saucepan and add the fruit. Bring to a boil, stirring constantly, then remove the mixture from the heat and place in a small bowl. When it has cooled down to room temperature, place it in the refrigerator for about an hour. If you want a smooth texture, you can put it into the blender for a few seconds before refrigerating it. For variety in flavor, add a little cinnamon or vanilla while the mixture is cooking.

Make Your Own Nut Butters

PEANUT BUTTER

ABOUT 1 ½ CUPS

Salt to taste (I suggest sea salt)

6 tablespoons light vegetable oil

3 cups raw peanuts, without the skins

To begin with, if you are using sea salt like I do, then you should mash some up with your mortar and pestle. Put half the oil into the blender, and then add about one-quarter of the nuts. Whiz it around in the blender until it becomes creamy. Add some more of the nuts, not too many, and whiz again. Add the rest of the oil and whiz again till it combines with the mixture. Now add some more of the peanuts and some salt (not too much salt). Whiz it around until it is smooth and then add the rest of the nuts.

Now, when you whiz it this time, don't do it too long and then you can have crunchy peanut butter, which is my favorite. If you don't like the crunchy kind, then let the blender go until it is the way you like it. Taste it and see if it needs any more salt. Use a rubber spatula to get it out so that you don't miss any. Eat what you can, and then refrigerate the rest. I suggest that you store it in a jar with a tight lid.

CASHEW BUTTER

ABOUT ¾ CUP

Salt to taste (again I suggest sea salt)

3 tablespoons light vegetable oil

1 ½ cups cashews

Mash up the salt if you are using sea salt. Put the oil into the blender and add some of the nuts. Whiz them around a bit until a creamy mixture forms. Now add a little salt and the rest of the nuts and whiz it to a creamy consistency. Taste to see if it is salty enough, and, if it is, remove it with a spatula and place it in a jar with a lid and refrigerate it.

COMBINATION NUT BUTTER

A very interesting nut spread can be prepared by combining a variety of nuts in the mixture, say, peanuts with almonds and cashews. If you ever do use almonds, remember to remove the skins first. This is called "blanching." You do it by pouring boiling water over the almonds and letting them stand for just a few seconds. Then drain off the water and remove the skins by rubbing the almonds between your thumb and forefinger. Dry them well to prevent the water from being absorbed by the almonds.

If you decide to make a combination nut spread, try this:

ABOUT ¾ CUP

½ cup blanched almonds　　*3 tablespoons light vegetable*
½ cup cashews　　　　　　　*oil*
½ cup walnuts　　　　　　　*Salt to taste (And I still suggest sea salt)*

Combine a few of each of the nuts with the oil in the blender and whiz them around. Keep adding a mixture of the nuts and blending them to a smooth consistency. Add a little salt and keep adding the nuts until they are all blended. Taste for saltiness and then either eat it or put it into a jar and refrigerate.

Definitions, Nutritions, and Prohibitions

Nuts and Seeds

Below is a simple list of the different types of nuts and seeds that I use in the dishes I prepare. I am only including the ones that I know and use. There are many others that I haven't felt the need to use, but they are available nonetheless for you to try if you are interested.

Although I love putting nuts and seeds into my cooked dishes, I try to eat as many raw as I can. Thus, I add nuts or seeds of some kind or another as a finishing touch to most salads that I make. I also place some on top of almost every sandwich I make or at least place some on the side.

NUTS

Almonds. Almonds are very nutritious, being high in vitamins, especially B vitamins: niacin, B_1 (thiamine), B_2 (riboflavin). They also contain iron, calcium, phosphorus, potassium, and are a very good source of protein. Almonds are high in unsaturated fats and they contain vegetable albumin, which is the easiest to digest of all available albumin. I use almonds in almost all my casseroles, cereals, and baking, and I eat them fresh a lot or on top of sandwiches.

Cashews. These nuts are unusual, because they grow outside of the fruit from which they come. This is great, because they are exposed to the sun and thus are a good source of vitamin D. They are also a good source of iron, thiamine, and of course protein. Because they are so expensive, I use them only in certain dishes, but I do serve them raw with cheese sandwiches, sometimes make cashew butter, and for a special treat make a sauce out of them for brown rice and vegetables.

Coconut. The milk and the meat of the coconut are both very valuable. They both have natural enzymes that aid in digestion. Coconut oil is a good substitute for butter, and it contains less fat. Coconut also contains calcium, iodine, and vitamin D, not to mention protein. Shredded coconut is good in different baked goods and cereals, and the milk is great to drink or use in cooking.

Peanuts. The most commonly used of all the nuts because they are so inexpensive. They are not nearly as nutritious as almonds or cashews and they contain a lot of fats. They sure do taste good, though, and they do have protein, niacin, and vitamin B. Peanuts can be pressed for oil for cooking. They also make great butter spreads, and in certain dishes are delicious.

Pecans. These are easily digested, and are high in unsaturated fats. They contain protein, calcium, iron, and vitamin A. They are great in baked goods, but they are at their best when eaten raw because they are in their natural state and there hasn't been any chemical change through heating. The fact is that all foods are at their nutritional best in their raw form because the vitamins and minerals, which are available naturally, haven't had a chance to get lost in a cooking process.

Walnuts. Walnuts are a good source of unsaturated fats, calcium, phosphorus, and of course protein. They are great in rice casseroles and different baked goods, but are at their best raw.

SEEDS

Flaxseed. These are high in unsaturated fats and contain iron, niacin, phosphorus, and protein. They are good in breads and can be added to cereals. I use them for sprouting, too.

Pumpkin seeds. I don't know too much about their nutritional value, but they sure are good. I toast them in a little oil in a covered pan over a high flame and they pop like popcorn. They are also good in cereals and salads.

Sesame seeds. These seeds are tremendously beneficial. They are high in unsaturated oils, calcium, and amino acids. They can be pressed to make a good cooking oil, and ground into a delicious spread by adding a little honey and oil. I also use them in breads and in cereals, plus in some of my cooked dishes, like Mushrooms in Sesame-Seed Sauce (page 92).

Sunflower seeds. These are a good source of vitamin D, and very high in protein. They contain calcium and phosphorus, which are good for bones and teeth. They are tasty eaten raw and in salads. I rarely cook them in anything, but I must say that they are good in oatmeal cookies, and toasted in a little oil.

About Eggs

I feel that I should say a few words about eggs. Within the health food diet there are various viewpoints about eggs. Some people say that they are good for you, and others are against the eating of eggs because they are so high in cholesterol and because eventually they can cause a great deal of trouble in blood circulation, among other problems. I myself do not eat eggs because I find that they are very difficult for me to digest. Whenever I eat an egg, I get an upset stomach, and a terrible sulfur aftertaste lingers for hours, along with great discomfort throughout my whole digestive tract. This is for real. It is said that whatever food value they have can be obtained in simpler forms through nuts and dairy products.

Now I must confess something. In all my attempts, I have not been able to eliminate eggs from my baking. I never eat them as a meal, but I cannot seem to create good enough bakery goods without them. Thus, although I try to avoid them, I do use them in most of the things that I make for dessert and in the little treats that I have lying around the kitchen for my friends. I try not to make too many things that contain eggs, but they do pop up in certain recipes where no substitution works. These recipes are included here because I love them so much. I have also included some recipes that do not contain eggs to give you an idea of the difference.

There is one bit of advice that I do have for you. It is that I think you should buy your eggs in a health food store you trust, instead of a regular supermarket. The store where I buy mine has brown eggs that come from healthy Rhode Island Red fathers and Barred Rock mothers. They are all brown eggs and are said to be almost 90 percent fertile. (Fertile eggs are supposed to be much more nutritious than nonfertile eggs.) The hens are allowed to run free and have total access to the roosters at all times. They are used for egg production for only a year and then sent to market. This prevents abuse of the hens, which often occurs on commercial egg farms where production is the main objective and to hell with the birds. Be sure and find out how the chickens you get your eggs from are treated, and what they are fed. They should be fed only the best and most natural feeds, free of chemicals, artificial vitamins, and animal by-products.

White eggs that you buy in the supermarket come from inferior birds that are raised only for egg laying and usually worn to the bone before they are left alone to retire. They are given steroids and all kinds of boosters just so they will be able to produce more eggs faster. The motto is definitely quantity, not quality.

About Flour

I am convinced that modern milling of flours removes most of the vitamins, minerals, and the valuable quality of the protein from the wheat. The reason for this is that all the food value is in the bran and wheat germ, both of which are removed before we even receive the flour.

In the milling process the bran (the outer coat of the wheat), which contains large amounts of vitamins and minerals, especially iron for the blood, and phosphorus for bones and the nervous system, is removed and set aside to sell to farmers for them to feed, because of its food value, to their livestock. How do you like that? They give the pigs foods of high value and then we are supposed to eat the pigs in order to get some secondhand food value. The system is crazy, but it does bring in more money for the grain farmers.

The wheat germ is removed next and sold to the farmers for their horses. Wheat germ is high in vitamin E, which is good for our hair and our skin. However, if we want to get it, we either have to take a vitamin supplement or else we, too, can buy wheat germ by itself at a great cost. Why not get it directly from the wheat itself? Why give the drug companies money for something that we can and should be able to get in its natural form?

By buying whole-grain flours we can be sure that we are getting all the food value we need from the flour. However, again it is important to remember that we should never buy more than we need. Seeing that the wheat germ and the bran are still present in the flours that we buy in the health food stores, it is likely that it can lose its value if it is allowed to sit around too long after it has been milled. As I have mentioned, at the store where I buy my flours they mill their own flours daily, and only as much as is needed to fill the day's demands. Thus I can be sure I am getting fresh whole grain, and, as long as I don't buy more than I need for, say, about five to ten days, I am guaranteed freshness.

Sugar Is a No-No

The information I have about sugar comes from a newsletter put out by the owner of the health food store where I shop. In it he says that white sugar (which is what everyone buys at his local supermarket) is 99.6 percent sucrose, which has no real food value because of the way it has been refined.

First off, sugar is grown with synthetic fertilizers and weed sprays, which I am trying to avoid in my food intake. Secondly, just before the harvesting of sugar cane all the fields are burned, which mistreats the soil. The refining process is done by huge machines, which boil, filter, and reduce the natural product to the form that is presented to us in the stores. All the molasses has been removed, and, I am sure, any nutritional value has been removed, too.

Brown sugar is just refined white sugar that has had some small amount of the molasses returned to it. Thus, I don't use the brown sugars, either.

I have found it very difficult to adjust to cooking without sugar, or should I say baking without it. That is where I really miss it. There are some recipes that I have had to totally abandon because there isn't a proper way to substitute honey in them. However, I feel that this is a simple adjustment to make for health's sake. Half the amount of honey will do in all of your recipes that call for sugar. If the recipe can't be converted satisfactorily, then forget it.

There are many different types of honey, and, to be totally honest with you, I haven't developed a total understanding of all of them yet. I have found out what the lightest-flavor honey is, and that was my most important goal. It is the wildflower honey. Clover is also light, but sometimes you can get a heavy batch and it can be very distinct in your dishes. I have been sticking to the wildflower.

If you still feel the need to use sugar, there are some that are made from maple syrup and dates, maple sugar and date sugar, but they are very expensive. I have used the maple in a few things, and it is really good, so I consider it a luxury.

About Water

I feel that I should give you some kind of an explanation about my thing for spring water. I love it, I think it is a wonder that it is available, and I think that it does make a difference in my cooking. However, there are many (and I do mean many) instances when I am caught dry in the spring water department. When this happens, the kitchen does not close down. Life goes on as usual, only whenever I need water for my cooking and I go to the sink I say to myself, Oooh Maureen, get yourself some spring water soon, girl, or you'll be sorry. Spring water is much clearer just to look at—clear as Paul Newman's eyes, right? The taste, too, is definitely far superior to the water that is processed and chemically treated for us by our friendly government workers. It can be expensive, but in these days, when the water we get from the taps is so full of strange chemicals put there to kill all the bacteria we get from the sewage we dump into our waterways, I feel the expense is worth it.

I try very hard to use spring water in all my foods that are cooked in water and have water in their recipes. However, when I am just washing vegetables or rinsing noodles or rice before cooking, I do use the tap water, only because I can't afford to be too frivolous. As far as drinking goes, there is no way that you could get me to drink the water from the tap unless I was taking a pill to maybe save my life. I guess this is a bit of an exaggeration, but I hope that you get the message.

The decision is always up to you. You may live in a rural area where the water isn't nearly as bad as the water we get in the cities, so you might well be satisfied with what you have. All I can say is that I am not satisfied with the water that I get from my tap, so I am cautious about using too much of it for consumption.

Why Use Brown Rice?

The story on brown rice is very similar to the one about flour. When you buy white rice you are buying the refined product that once was brown. When it goes through the refining process most, if not all, of the vitamins and minerals are removed. Brown rice has all these vitamins and minerals, and, although it does take longer to cook, it is well worth it as far as I am concerned.

Don't Peel Your Vegetables . . .

When I was a little girl, my mother told me to peel all the vegetables before eating them. I listened to her like all good girls do only to find out later that there are a lot of minerals and vitamins in the skins of most of the vegetables I was peeling. I just want to make sure that you know that if you wash your vegetables very well and scrub them with your hands or a vegetable brush (depending on what you prefer), that you are doing all you need to do in order to prepare your vegetables for eating.

For appearance's sake, it is a good idea to cut away any bruises or scars from vegetables and fruits when you are preparing them. The only vegetables that I peel now are eggplant, avocado, onions, cucumbers (sometimes), potatoes (sometimes), tomatoes (sometimes), beets, and of course I take the peas from the pods. Although fresh pea pods like you get in Chinese food are a trip.

I strongly suggest that at any given visit to the store you don't buy more vegetables than you need for two days. For the best results, they should always be bought fresh and cooked fresh. When you get home from the store with your vegetables, clean them right away and dry them well. They can then be put into your vegetable cooler ready for use.

Why I Use Stainless Steel and Porcelain

It is my belief that Teflon is safe as long as it isn't heated. When it is heated, it gives off toxic gases that we can inhale if we are using it. This conclusion came to me after reading an article by Linda Clark in *Let's Live* magazine. I'm not sure which issue it was, because I borrowed it from a friend of mine. It was either in 1970 or early 1971 (I'm pretty sure that it was in 1970). The word "Teflon" is the trade name for fluorocarbon resins. Those resins often scrape off or even chip while you are using the pans. Where do you suppose those little resins go? My guess is that they go into your stomach—and I don't believe that they are too easily digestible, do you?

If you are cooking with aluminum, there is a similar threat. Your saliva is an alkaline substance that is swallowed along with the food you eat. When food is cooked in aluminum, small compounds of the alum unite with the food. When you eat the food it unites with your saliva and then you swallow it. This can produce a gas in your digestive tract, causing discomfort and possibly doing more damage than that. This information came from the *Journal of Natural Living*.

With stainless steel and porcelain I believe that there is no threat of these things occurring. That is why I choose to use them in my cooking.

II

Recipes

Breads and Rice

Breads

I feel that I owe you a special apology here, because I have no great recipe to give you for an everyday bread. There is a reason for this, and I hope that you will accept it. There is one recipe for bread baking that I use constantly, but I can't give it to you. It was given to me by my girl friend Sandee, who won't allow me to use it in my cookbook. In fact, she won't even allow me to give it to any of my other friends. Now I know that this may seem strange, but it is Sandee's trip. She found the recipe somewhere, and it is really a winner, and I sure had to do a number on her head in order to get her to give it to me. The only way that she would give it to me was if I swore not to give it to anyone. Well, not being able to give it to anyone certainly means that I am not able to use it in my book.

But I just had a great idea: why don't you write and ask her for the recipe? Tell her some far-out story about how you have an undernourished family who needs fresh-baked bread and you don't have much time for baking, and that you heard that she was in possession of a far-out quick bread recipe that was very nutritious and delicious. Offer her a bribe or something. Send her a quarter or a pretty drawing. (Drawings are her weakness. I've never seen her say no to a nice drawing.) Her address is 234 Lily Street, San

Francisco, California 94102, and her last name is Hicks. Don't tell her where you got her name.

I can't pretend to make up other recipes, because there just aren't any others that I have tried or tested. Hers is so good and you can vary it so easily that I have never wanted to try and find another to take its place or alternate it with.

However, what I can give you are my own recipes for special breads that you can make every now and then. They are all tasty, and there is no reason why you can't make them more often if you want. I like the simple bread for daily use because it doesn't detract from my meals.

CHALLAH

2 LOAVES

4½–5½ cups sifted all-purpose flour
1½ tablespoons honey
1½ tablespoons salt
1 tablespoon undissolved yeast
½ cup milk

½ cup plus 1 teaspoon spring water
¼ cup butter
Pinch of saffron
4 eggs
Sesame seeds

In a large bowl, thoroughly mix 1¼ cups of the flour, the honey, salt, and yeast.

Combine the milk, ½ cup water, butter, and saffron in a saucepan and heat just till warm; the butter need not melt. Gradually add it to the flour mixture in the bowl and beat at least 2 minutes. Add 3 eggs, 1 egg white (save the yolk), and ½ cup flour, to make it thick. Beat 2 minutes. Now stir in enough flour to make a soft dough. Turn out on a lightly floured bread board and knead 8 to 10 minutes. (I hate kneading dough. It always sticks to my hands and looks awful. Every time I come to the kneading I'm afraid to go on because I'm sure by the way it looks that it will be a boo-boo.

So don't worry if you think so, too. It is very interesting to me how when our mothers were young they were so busy relating to being "modern" that they never would have thought of baking their own bread. I guess they saw all the work their mothers used to do and figured that it was crazy. They were right—isn't being crazy fun?)

Place in a greased bowl, turning to grease the top of the dough. Cover and let rise till double in size—about 1 hour.

Punch down. Next you should shape it into loaves. Here's what I do: I divide the dough into 2 balls. Then I divide the balls into 3 parts and roll them into long strips and then braid them, sealing the ends securely. Place on a greased cookie sheet. Beat the remaining egg yolk with 1 teaspoon cold water. Brush over the loaves and sprinkle with sesame seeds. Let rise 1 more hour. (When you have dough to rise, I suggest that you put it into the oven with just the pilot light on; it seems to work for me.) Bake at 400° for 30 minutes.

ORGANIC BAGELS

ABOUT 1 DOZEN

2 cups spring water
1 cup butter
1 cup whole-wheat flour, sifted well
1 cup whole-wheat pastry

flour, sifted well
1 tablespoon honey
½ teaspoon salt
5 eggs

Boil the water; while it is boiling, add the butter and let it melt. When the butter is completely melted, add the two flours, honey, and salt. Mix till a ball forms. Remove from the heat and add the eggs, one at a time, beating the mixture after each addition.

Moisten your hands and form the dough into little balls, placing them on an ungreased cookie sheet about 2 inches apart. Dampen your hands and stick your finger through each ball, making a hole. Thus you have bagels. Bake at 400° for 25 minutes.

DATE-NUT LOAF

1 MEDIUM LOAF

½ pound dates, chopped
1½ cups boiling spring water
2½ cups sifted whole-wheat pastry flour
2½ teaspoons baking powder
¼ teaspoon salt

1 egg
2 tablespoons melted butter
½ cup honey
1 teaspoon vanilla extract
1 cup chopped nuts (Mix them—a little almonds, walnuts, pecans, etc.)
Raisins (optional)

Chop the dates and add them to the boiling water. Boil about 3–5 minutes and then set aside in a bowl to cool. (It is always better to pour something into a bowl to cool rather than let it cool in the pan in which you cooked it. This way you don't have to wait for the pan to cool before the mixture can start to cool.)

Combine and sift together the dry ingredients. Beat the egg and then add it to the date mixture and stir. Add the date mixture to the dry ingredients and mix. Add the melted butter, honey, and vanilla and mix again. Blend in the nuts and the raisins, if you want them. Mix and then turn into a greased loaf pan and bake at 325° for about 1 hour and 15 minutes.

CRANBERRY-ORANGE BREAD

1 MEDIUM LOAF

2 cups whole-wheat pastry flour

½ teaspoon baking soda
½ teaspoon salt

3 teaspoons baking powder
Rind of 1 orange
¾ cup fresh orange juice
1 egg, slightly beaten
⅓ cup honey
2 tablespoons melted butter

2 tablespoons hot spring water
1 cup chopped nuts
1 cup raw cranberries, cut in half
Raisins (optional)

Sift the flour and then sift the other dry ingredients into the flour. Stir in the orange rind. In another bowl, combine the egg, honey, orange juice, melted butter, and water. Fold the egg mixture into the dry ingredients, and add the nuts, cranberries, and raisins, if you want some of them, too. Turn into a greased loaf pan and bake at 350° for 50 to 60 minutes.

CORN CRUNCHIES
ABOUT 1½–2 DOZEN (DEPENDING ON HOW FLAT YOU POUND THEM)

2 cups whole-wheat pastry flour
½ cup cornmeal
1 teaspoon salt

Spring water (enough to make a bread-dough consistency)
Sesame seeds or poppy seeds

Sift the flour and cornmeal well, and then sift them together with the salt. Add the water. I don't know why, but the amount varies from time to time. Start with 1 cup and add more, slowly, till the dough is elastic-like. Knead it for 10 to 20 minutes, depending on your patience. I usually make it about 10 minutes if I'm lucky, but then my crunchies are never as good as those of my friends, who really get into the kneading.

Divide the dough into little balls and roll each one to a thin roundish sheet. (It will probably end up looking like a taco shell before it has been folded.) Place the rolled-out dough balls on an ungreased cookie sheet and sprinkle with sesame seeds or poppy seeds and bake at 350° for 10 to 12 minutes.

For variety, you can substitute rye flour for the cornmeal and sprinkle with caraway seeds and ground salt.

SESAME ROUNDS

ABOUT 3 DOZEN CRACKERS

1 *cup sifted whole-wheat pastry flour*	2 *tablespoons milk*
¾ *teaspoon salt*	¼ *cup plus 2 tablespoons sesame seeds*
⅓ *cup softened butter*	1 *cup shredded cheese*
2 *tablespoons chopped chives*	*Garlic salt (optional)*

Sift your flour with the salt. Combine the butter with the chives in a small bowl and blend well. Add the flour and the milk alternately until they are blended well with the butter mixture. Add the ¼ cup sesame seeds and the cheese and mix together well. Take balls of the dough and roll them into small cylinders about 1 inch in thickness. I usually end up with 4 or 5 cylinder rolls. Now wrap them up in some waxed paper and refrigerate them for at least 3 hours. They should get nice and firm. The firmer they get, the easier they will be for you to slice when you go to bake them.

When you are ready to bake them, remove them from the refrigerator and slice them as thinly as you can. (Sometimes I can get them very thin, and then there are days when I am super clumsy and they come out at least ½ inch thick. It isn't any big deal, just when you are going to serve them to guests before dinner it is nice if they look thin and dainty. Also, the thinner they are the crisper they will be. Don't take them out to bake until your guests have already begun to arrive. Then they will be nice and warm when you serve them.) As you slice them, place them on a greased cookie sheet and then sprinkle them with a little garlic salt and the remaining sesame seeds, if you want.

These will change in flavor depending on the type of cheese you choose to use. The heaviest I use is sharp Cheddar. It is my favorite, but when I just want a subtle treat I use Monterey Jack or Swiss and leave the garlic salt off for sure.

You can also vary them by adding different dried spices in place of the chopped chives. I use basil with the Jack cheese and parsley with the Swiss.

Rice

CORRECT BROWN RICE

ABOUT 4 CUPS COOKED RICE

I think it is important to note that brown rice has all the vitamins and minerals that have been refined out of white rice. *And always rinse rice before you cook it.*

2 *cups spring water*
1 *cup brown rice*
¼ *teaspoon salt*
1 *tablespoon soy sauce (optional; I always put a little* *soy sauce in my rice no matter what I am making. I like what it does to the flavor)*

Place the water in a 2-quart saucepan. Add the rice and salt and stir around a little. Place a high flame under the pan and bring to a boil. As soon as the rice comes to a boil, reduce the flame and cover the pan. Allow the rice to simmer for about 45 minutes. Be sure to check it after about 40 minutes and every few minutes thereafter until it is just the way you like it. You can always add a little more water if it becomes too dry for your taste.

One thing I would like to add is that I have found that using a stainless-steel pot makes much better rice than any other pan I have. The rice always comes out fluffy and soft.

HERB RICE

ABOUT 4 CUPS COOKED RICE

If you are going to use the rice as a side dish instead of just under the main course, it is sometimes nice to add some herbs when you start to cook it.

2 *cups spring water*
1 *cup brown rice*
¼ *teaspoon salt*
1 *teaspoon mixed herbs (I usually use basil and marjoram)*

1 *teaspoon chopped parsley*
1 *tablespoon soy sauce (optional)*
Wheat-germ oil or butter (optional)

Place all the ingredients in a 2-quart saucepan and stir them around a bit. Then bring the rice to a boil over a high flame. (A flame trivet will be very helpful in making rice, as it is in so many sensitive dishes.) When the rice starts to boil, reduce the flame to simmer and cover the pan. The rice should be ready in about 40 to 45 minutes.

If you are going to make this a side dish, add a little wheat-germ oil and stir it in very well right before serving. Butter is good, too, but it isn't as good for you as the wheat-germ oil.

ALMOND FRIED RICE

SERVES 4 (OR 2 HUNGRY PEOPLE)

4 *cups cooked Correct Brown Rice (page 47)*
1 *medium onion, chopped*
1 *cup chopped celery*
1 *large carrot, chopped or thinly sliced (I chop it in*

uneven chunks because it looks good that way)
1 *cup sliced mushrooms*
Some lettuce leaves, torn up
1 ½ *cups chopped almonds*
Light vegetable oil

Please remember that any vegetable can be added to most of my dishes. Just because I haven't mentioned it doesn't mean you can't use it. Please satisfy yourself, not the recipe!

While the rice is cooking, get all your vegetables together, and when the rice is finished, set it aside. When all the vegetables are ready, steam them in a steamer or in a wok for just a few minutes, remembering to cook the toughest vegetables first. When they start to become tender, add them to the rice, along with the almonds, and mix well.

Now place a little oil in a frying pan and put the rice mixture in to fry, a little at a time. Stir occasionally, and when the rice begins to crisp a bit it is ready. Serve it with some soy sauce on the side. I also fry up some Tofu (page 58), and serve them together.

Soups

It is hard to approximate serving suggestions, because I usually serve big bowls of soup. I guess it is me, but no one ever eats just one small cup of anything at my house.

Soup is good for dinner, and if there is any left over you can have it for lunch the next day.

VEGETABLE SOUP

ABOUT 8 SERVINGS

2 onions, diced
3 tablespoons butter
3 quarts spring water
2 carrots, sliced
1 cup lima beans, soaked
   overnight
1 cup peas
¼ pound green beans
1 cup chopped cabbage
2 turnips, diced

1 cup chopped celery
1 tablespoon salt
½ teaspoon pepper
¼ teaspoon sweet basil
1 clove garlic, minced
2 potatoes, peeled and
   chopped
4 tomatoes, peeled and
   chopped

Sauté the onions in the butter. Put the water in a large pan and add the onions, carrots, lima beans, peas, green beans, cabbage, turnips, celery, and whatever is in season at the time you are making the soup. (The object is to create variety. If asparagus is in season and cheap, why not add a little of it? Corn cut off the cob could be a nice addition one summer evening. It is really all up to you.) Add your herbs and spices now. (The same holds true here, too. If there is something you really love and I haven't used it, don't hesitate. I have a cousin who would put dill in everything that came out of the kitchen if he could. That's his taste, and, although I hate dill, I understand his thing for it.) Add the potatoes, and the tomatoes. Cook over low heat for about 40 minutes, checking to see that the vegetables are cooked to your satisfaction.

BEAN AND BARLEY SOUP

ABOUT 6 SERVINGS

1 *cup lima beans, soaked overnight in spring water*	2 *carrots, sliced*
	2 *onions, chopped*
⅓ *cup barley, soaked overnight in spring water*	2 *teaspoons salt*
	½ *teaspoon pepper*
2 *quarts spring water*	¼ *teaspoon garlic salt*
⅓ *cup soy sauce*	1 *teaspoon chopped parsley*

After soaking overnight, rinse the beans and the barley. Place in a large soup pan and pour in the water and the soy sauce. Stir a little, then add the carrots, onions, salt, pepper, garlic salt, and parsley. Mix it up a little, and simmer it for about 3 hours, stirring occasionally. Check the seasoning and serve hot, with some nice home-baked bread.

BEET BORSCHT

ABOUT 6 SERVINGS

2 quarts spring water
6 beets, washed and peeled
1 onion, finely chopped
1 tablespoon salt
¼ cup lemon juice

1 ½ tablespoons honey
1 teaspoon cider vinegar (optional)
Sour cream

Put the water, beets, onion, and salt in a pan. Bring to a boil, reduce the heat, and cook over a medium flame for 1 hour. Add the lemon juice, honey, and vinegar and simmer for 30 minutes more.

Remove the beets from the soup. Cut 5 of the beets into strips. Cut the other beet into small chunks, put the chunks in the blender, and purée them. Add the puréed beet to the soup and stir. Add ¼ cup sour cream and mix. Stir in the strips, pour the soup in a bowl, and put it in the refrigerator to chill for about 3 hours.

Serve the soup cold, with a scoop of sour cream on top.

CABBAGE BORSCHT

ABOUT 4 BIG SERVINGS

9 cups shredded cabbage (if you mix red and green cabbage, use it at a two-to-one ratio, using more of the green)
2 onions, chopped
¼ cup melted butter
2 tablespoons whole-wheat flour
4 cups spring water

6 tomatoes, peeled
1 tablespoon salt
½ teaspoon pepper
1 tablespoon honey
2 tablespoons lemon juice
1 teaspoon cider vinegar
¼–½ cup raisins (optional)
2 teaspoons caraway seeds
Sour cream (optional)

In a large pan cook the cabbage and the onions in the butter. Toss it around a lot, being careful not to let the vegetables brown at all. Thus you should be using a very low flame. Sprinkle the flour over the vegetables and stir. Increase the heat and pour the water in slowly, stirring constantly until the soup begins to boil. Add the tomatoes, salt, pepper, honey, lemon juice, vinegar, raisins, and caraway seeds. Cook over medium heat for about 1 hour, stirring frequently. Every once in a while test the seasoning.

Serve it hot, with a scoop of sour cream in it if you want. That is the way some people do it, but not me. As much as I love sour cream, I find it definitely out of place in this soup.

POTATO-LEEK SOUP

ABOUT 5 SERVINGS

¼ cup butter

4 leeks, thoroughly washed and finely sliced

3 potatoes, peeled and thinly sliced

½ teaspoon celery salt

2 teaspoons salt

2 teaspoon chopped parsley

¼ teaspoon pepper

6 cups spring water

2 cups milk

Melt the butter in a saucepan. Add the leeks and cook slowly for a few minutes, then add the potatoes, celery salt, salt, 1 teaspoon of the parsley, the pepper, and the water. Cook over a low heat until the potatoes are soft and begin to blend into the water. Actually, they have to get pretty mushy. It takes about 1 hour. Add the milk and stir well. (You can put it in the blender if you want to. I don't, because I like it when I can eat the leeks whole. I know I could take them out before I use the blender, but I'm too lazy to do it usually.) Add the remaining parsley now, and simmer for 20 minutes.

SPLIT-PEA FILL-ER-UP SOUP

6 BIG SERVINGS (CAN FEED 8 OR 10)

2 cups split peas

2½ quarts spring water (This will make a very thick soup, so if you want a thinner soup use 3 quarts of water instead of 2½)

6-10 carrots, washed but not peeled

2 bunches leeks (thoroughly cleaned) or 2 onions (or both, if you are an onion freak like me)

Tarragon

Rosemary

Marjoram

Basil

Celery salt

Parsley

2 tablespoons salt

1 tablespoon pepper

Put the split peas in a pan and cover them with the water. Add the sliced vegetables and herbs and spices next. (Add as much of each of the herbs and spices as you like. I use from ½ to 1 teaspoon of each.) Bring to a boil and allow it to boil about 10 minutes. Be careful not to let it bubble over, because not only will it make a mess but you will loose the herbs and spices. Now reduce the heat to simmer. (I hope that you have a gas stove, because that is how I cook, and it is better for me than an electric.) Anyway, after you reduce the heat to simmer you should allow it to cook at least 3 hours, remembering to stir it at least every 15 minutes or so.

CREAM OF ASPARAGUS SOUP

ABOUT 4 SERVINGS

1 pound asparagus

3 cups salted spring water

1 large onion, chopped

¼ cup butter

1½ teaspoons salt

½ teaspoon pepper

¼ teaspoon garlic salt

½ teaspoon celery salt

2 teaspoons chopped parsley

2 tablespoons whole-wheat flour

1 cup milk or cream

¼ cup sliced almonds

Wash the asparagus, then cut off the tops and save, chopping up the rest of the stalks. Cook the chopped stalks in the salted spring water for 10 to 15 minutes, until tender.

Lightly sauté the onion in half the butter and then add to the cooked asparagus. Stir and cook until soft over low heat. Add the salt, pepper, garlic salt, celery salt, and 1 teaspoon of the parsley. Put the soup in the blender and whiz until the ingredients are blended well. Make a cream sauce by melting the remaining butter, stirring in the flour with a whisk, adding the milk, and stirring well until the sauce thickens. Add to the soup and stir. Drop in the asparagus tips and the sliced almonds and simmer for 20 to 30 minutes.

CREAM OF CELERY SOUP

2 BIG SERVINGS

2 cups spring water
2 cups chopped celery
¾ cup chopped onion
5 tablespoons butter
1 ½ teaspoons chopped parsley
3 tablespoons whole-wheat

flour or arrowroot starch
1 ½ cups milk
1 ½ teaspoons salt
¼ teaspoon pepper
garlic powder (optional)
2 cups sliced mushrooms
(optional)

Put the water on to boil. Sauté the celery and the onion in 2 tablespoons of the butter. Add the vegetables to the water and stir well. Cook over medium low heat for 2 hours, stirring from time to time. Purée in the blender and return to the pan. Add the chopped parsley.

Make a white sauce by melting the remaining butter in a pan and adding the flour or starch, blending with a wire whisk. Add the milk and stir well until the sauce begins to thicken. Add the salt, pepper, and a little garlic powder if you desire. Pour into the celery mixture and stir well. For additional flavor, I sauté about 2 cups of sliced mushrooms and put them in the soup right before I serve it.

CREAM OF MUSHROOM SOUP

ABOUT 4 SERVINGS

¾ *pound mushrooms, sliced*
5 *tablespoons butter*
1 *onion, chopped*
⅓ *cup chopped celery*
3 *cups spring water*
2 *teaspoons chopped parsley*

1 *teaspoon salt*
¼ *teaspoon pepper*
¼ *teaspoon garlic salt*
2 *tablespoons whole-wheat pastry flour*
1½ *cups milk or cream*

Sauté the mushrooms in 2 tablespoons of the butter. Remove from the pan and set aside. Sauté the onion and celery in the butter left in the pan, adding 1 more tablespoon, if necessary.

Put the water on to boil. Add the onion and three-quarters of the mushrooms, plus 1 teaspoon of the parsley, the salt, pepper, and garlic salt. Cover and cook over low heat for 20 minutes. Stir it up, then put the soup in the blender and purée it. Return it to the pan and add the rest of the sautéed mushrooms.

Make a white sauce by melting the remaining 2 tablespoons butter, stirring in the flour with a whisk, adding the milk, and stirring well till it thickens. Add the sauce to the soup and mix well. Add the remaining parsley and simmer for another 15 minutes. Before serving, test the seasoning to make sure it is right. No recipe can be perfect to everyone's taste. Add whatever you may think is necessary in order to please you and yours.

Nuts, Seeds, and Beans

LENTILS AND NUTS

ABOUT 4 SERVINGS

3 cups lentils, cooked and puréed in the blender

1 ½ cups nuts (I use a little of various types—almonds, walnuts, cashews, etc.)

½ cup ground sunflower seeds

¼ cup chopped onion

¼ cup wheat-germ oil—or whatever oil you want to use

½ cup rye cracker crumbs or your favorite bread crumbs

1 teaspoon sage

1 teaspoon salt

½ teaspoon celery salt

1 tablespoon soy sauce

In a large bowl mix the cooked, puréed lentils with the nuts, which have been chopped up a little, and the ground sunflower seeds. Sauté the onion in a little of the oil until it is tender. Add the cracker crumbs, sage, salt, and celery salt and cook, stirring, over low heat for a few minutes. Add the cracker crumb mixture to the lentil mixture and mix in the soy sauce and the remaining oil. Bake in a 350° oven for about 1 hour. This dish is also good with a little fried Tofu (page 58) on the side.

TOFU

ABOUT 2–3 CUPS

Tofu is soybean curd cheese. It can be bought in most health food stores, which is the way I usually get it. However, it can be made, so I am going to give you a quick recipe for it in case you want to make your own.

I fry it with a few sautéed vegetables sometimes for lunch, and usually put it into all my Oriental-type dishes in chunks. It is very good for you, for it is made of soybean products, which are full of protein.

1 cup soy flour
1 quart spring water

3 tablespoons fresh-squeezed
   lemon juice
½ teaspoon salt

In your blender, mix the flour with the spring water until they are well blended. If you have only a 1-quart limit on your blender, which is the usual size, do only half at a time. Be sure to put the water in first and then add the flour. This will help guarantee that all the flour will be dissolved. When the flour and the water are combined, place the mixture in your double boiler and double-boil it for 20 minutes. Remove it from the heat and add the lemon juice and the salt right away. Stir it gently and let it stand to cool for about 30 minutes, or until the cheese has formed. When the cheese has formed, strain it through your colander lined with cheesecloth.

This cheese can be substituted for cottage cheese in any recipe you may have. You can also scramble it like eggs with some vegetables in it.

ORGANIC YENTA'S "MEAT LOAF"

ABOUT 5 SERVINGS

5 cups cooked soybeans
½ cup tamari sauce

¾ cup light vegetable oil
½ teaspoon cayenne pepper

½ teaspoon chili powder
1 teaspoon dry mustard
3½ cloves garlic, chopped
¾ teaspoon ground cumin
1½ teaspoons dill weed
1½ teaspoons celery salt

1½ teaspoons ground thyme
3 cups cooked brown rice
2–3 tablespoons lecithin
1–2 chopped onions
1 carrot, grated
½ cup chopped celery

Grind up the soybeans in the blender, then mix well with the tamari sauce, oil, herbs, and spices. Add the rice, lecithin, chopped onions, grated carrot, and chopped celery and mix well.

Put into a loaf pan and bake at 350° for 1 hour.

People who don't like meat loaf will really like this. People who do like meat loaf will point out that it's not the same thing, which it's not. So call it something else, like "Soybean Surprise," when you serve it to them and they'll be happy.

If you don't want a loaf, you can shape the mixture into patties and either fry or broil them with a little Monterey Jack cheese on top.

MOMMY'S BAKED BEANS

4 OR 5 SERVINGS

2 cups beans, soaked overnight (I use lima beans or navy beans)
Enough water to cover the beans in the pan

2 onions, sliced
2 cups tomatoes, peeled and chopped
2 tablespoons salt
1 teaspoon pepper

Place the beans in the water (I hope you are using spring water? Remember it's for your own good). Add the onions, tomatoes, salt, and pepper to the pan and bring to a boil. Boil for 10 minutes, then reduce the heat to low and cook for 3 hours. Be sure that there is enough water to prevent burning. You want to encourage thickening, but not to make the beans so thick that something happens on the bottom of the pan.

ROASTED SOYBEANS

ABOUT 4 CUPS

This is a great, munchy item that is pure protein. It isn't hard to do, and once you've got them done just watch how quickly they disappear.

Salt   *Spring water to cover*
  2 cups soybeans   *Garlic powder (optional)*

I use sea salt, which I believe to be the most natural form of salt —it has had nothing done to it except some drying. So when I make these soybeans I first have to mash up some salt with the mortar and pestle.

Put the soybeans into a bowl and cover them with spring water and put a little salt in the water. Soak the soybeans in the refrigerator overnight.

Next morning, drain and rinse the soybeans and then cook them in the water you soaked them in, with 2 more teaspoons salt, for about 1½ to 2 hours, at a fairly high heat but below boiling. Drain and rinse them again and then let them dry for a while (about 15 minutes).

Now spread the beans out over a cookie sheet and put them into a 375° oven for 50 to 60 minutes, or until they turn golden brown. Sprinkle them with a little salt as soon as they come out of the oven. For a little change you can add some garlic powder to the salt before you sprinkle it over the roasted soybeans. When they are cool, place them in a tightly covered jar.

LIMA BAKE

4–5 SERVINGS

1 cup onion, chopped
1 clove garlic, minced
2 cups chopped celery
½ cup chopped green pepper
1½ cups tomatoes
Arrowroot starch or flour

2 cups lima beans, soaked overnight in spring water
1½ cups cracker or bread crumbs
1 teaspoon salt
Basil or marjoram (optional)

Sauté the onion, garlic, celery, and green pepper in the olive oil. Purée the tomatoes in the blender with a little arrowroot starch or flour to make it thick (start out with 1 or 2 teaspoons and work up from there until the desired thickness is obtained). Mix the tomatoes with the vegetables, bread crumbs, and salt. Add a little basil or marjoram if you like; I do. Place in a casserole and bake at 375° for 45 minutes.

CHILI BEANS

ABOUT 4 SERVINGS

1 cup dried kidney beans, soaked overnight
1 cup dried soybeans, soaked overnight
5 very ripe tomatoes, peeled and chopped
1 large onion, chopped
1 clove garlic, minced
2 tablespoons butter
Boiling spring water to cover
1 red pepper, chopped

1 green pepper, chopped
1 cup sunflower seeds
1 teaspoon salt
¼ teaspoon pepper
1 teaspoon paprika
¼ teaspoon chili powder or cayenne pepper (I use the chili powder)
1½ tablespoons whole-wheat flour, approximately

Soak the beans separately overnight. In the morning, rinse them off and cook them, separately again, in fresh spring water. The kidney beans take only about 20 minutes to cook, but the soybeans have to cook at least 1½ hours. When they are done, drain them well and put them into a deep casserole and add the tomatoes, onions, garlic, and butter. Toss everything around together, and then cover it with enough boiling spring water to cover everything.

Place the dish, covered, into a slow oven (about 250°) for about 4 to 5 hours, but don't just leave it there; it is important that you check the dish every hour at least to make sure that there is enough water in the dish. Otherwise, the beans will begin to stick and burn. An hour before you are going to serve the casserole, add the peppers, sunflower seeds, and all the spices and stir them in. Don't forget to make sure that there is enough water. Right before serving, add the flour by sprinkling it over the mixture and stirring it in to form a paste with the juices. Add more flour, if necessary.

Noodle Dishes

MACARONI AND CHEESE

ABOUT 4 SERVINGS

1 large onion, chopped
1 cup chopped green pepper
6 tablespoons butter
2 cups sliced mushrooms
2 cups sesame macaroni
Salted spring water
2 tablespoons whole-wheat flour
1¼ cups milk, approximately
2 cups shredded cheese (I use Cheddar most of the time, but once in a while I do half and half with Monterey Jack)
½ teaspoon salt
Pepper (optional)
2 tablespoons chopped parsley
½ cup sunflower seeds
Tiny handful caraway seeds (more like a pinchful)

Sauté the onions and green pepper in 3 tablespoons of the butter, then remove from the skillet. Add the mushrooms and sauté in the butter remaining in the pan. Cook the sesame macaroni in salted spring water till it is just beginning to become tender.

Make a cream sauce by melting 2 tablespoons of the butter, stirring in the flour with a whisk, and then adding the milk, stirring well. When the sauce begins to thicken, remove from the heat and stir in the cheese, salt, pepper (if you want some), and the parsley.

Stir constantly until the cheese melts and the sauce is smooth. If it gets too thick, add another ¼ cup milk and stir it in well. Add the sunflower and caraway seeds to the cream sauce and then the vegetables. Put the remaining 1 tablespoon butter on the noodles and stir it around, then add the noodles to the cheese sauce. Mix it all up, then place it in a casserole and bake for 20 minutes at 350°.

COTTAGE-CHEESE CASSEROLE

ABOUT 4 SERVINGS

2 cups whole-wheat noodles
Salted spring water
1 ½ cups cottage cheese
2 cups sour cream
½ cup chopped green onion
1 teaspoon salt

¼ teaspoon pepper
1 teaspoon chopped parsley
1 cup rye cracker crumbs
¼ cup sesame seeds
2 tablespoons butter
½ cup grated Cheddar cheese

Cook the noodles in salted spring water until they are slightly tender. Mix the noodles with the cottage cheese, sour cream, onion, salt, pepper, and parsley in a bowl and then turn it into a casserole dish. Brown the cracker crumbs and sesame seeds in the butter and then sprinkle them on top of the casserole. Bake at 350° for 30 minutes. Remove from the oven, sprinkle the grated cheese on top, and return to the oven for another 10 minutes.

CHEESE KREPLACH

4–6 SERVINGS

DOUGH

2 eggs
¼ cup spring water
2 cups sifted whole-wheat
  pastry flour

Salt
2 tablespoons butter
Sour cream

Beat the eggs with the water. Add the flour slowly, mixing until you can form a ball stiff enough to roll out. Roll out the dough on a floured bread board to a ¼-inch thickness. Cut into squares and put a tablespoon of the filling (see below) on each square. Fold diagonally and pinch the corners and sides together. Drop into boiling salted water and cook about 20 minutes. Remove and fry in a skillet in the butter till brown on both sides.

Serve with sour cream.

FILLING

½ *pound cottage cheese*	¼ *teaspoon salt*
¼ *pound farmer's cheese*	¼ *teaspoon honey*
1 *egg*	¼ *teaspoon cinnamon*

Mix all the ingredients together and it's ready to put onto the dough.

VEGETARIAN KREPLACH

4–6 SERVINGS

1 *cup chopped mushrooms*	¼ *cup sour cream* (*optional*)
½ *cup chopped onion*	2 *eggs*
½ *cup chopped green pepper*	½ *cup spring water*
¼ *cup butter*	2 *cups sifted whole-wheat*
1 *pound cottage cheese*	*pastry flour*

Sauté the vegetables in the butter and mix with the cottage cheese. (You can also add about ¼ cup sour cream, too, if you'd like. I do.) Set the filling aside.

Make a dough by beating the eggs with the water and then slowly adding the flour, mixing until a ball, stiff enough to roll out, forms. Roll out the dough on a floured surface until it is about ¼ inch thick. Now cut it into little squares and place a tablespoon of the filling into the center of each. Fold the squares diagonally and press the edges together. Place them on a greased cookie sheet and bake them at 350° until they are brown, about 20 minutes.

NOODLES AND CABBAGE

ABOUT 5 SERVINGS

4 *cups shredded cabbage, preferably green*
1 *teaspoon salt*
½ *cup butter*
¼ *teaspoon pepper*
¾ *teaspoon honey*
3 *cups cooked noodles (I use*

spinach noodles in this one for a special flavor. If you want something a little gentler, use sesame noodles)
½ *cup sliced almonds*

Mix the cabbage with the salt and toss around a little. Let it stand for about an hour, then drain off the liquid. Melt the butter in a large skillet. Add the cabbage, pepper, and honey and cook over low heat for about 45 minutes, stirring frequently. When the cabbage is slightly browned, add the cooked noodles and toss. Add the almonds, mix, and serve.

By the way, I always use more nuts than I say in my recipes. I'm trying to be reasonable with you, but if you're anything like me you'll want to use more, too. I rationalize it by telling myself that the nuts are good protein, which of course is true.

LOKSHEN KUGEL

4–6 SERVINGS

I have always been a great lokshen kugel fan, but this new creation really knocks me out. I use spinach noodles in mine, but you can use whole-wheat or soy noodles. The spinach noodles make quite a distinctive difference. (Also, you can save money if you buy the noodles by the pound in bulk. This is what I do at the store where I shop. If you can shop in bulk, then use about 2½ cups of dry noodles.)

1 *package or 2½ cups dry spinach noodles*
Salted spring water
½ cup butter
¼ pound mushrooms (or more, according to your own personal taste), sliced

1 *pound creamed cottage cheese*
¼ cup sour cream
Salt and pepper to taste
¼ pound walnuts (or more, according to your own personal taste), chopped

Boil the noodles in salted spring water. (As far as I'm concerned, there is no set time for cooking noodles. I test them with a wooden spoon I have that is special for noodles. When they are soft enough for my taste, then I know they are done.) Drain well, rinse, and put in a bowl with 6 tablespoons of the butter and mix around.

While the noodles were boiling you should have sautéed the mushrooms in the remaining 2 tablespoons butter.

Mix the cottage cheese, sour cream, salt and pepper to taste, mushrooms, and walnuts. Pour over the noodles and mix around. Now pour into a casserole dish and bake at 350° for 30 minutes.

I hope you like it. As a main dish this should serve four people Jewish-mother style, or six people, regular.

MOTHER'S LOKSHEN KUGEL

4–6 SERVINGS

2½ *cups sesame noodles*
Salted spring water
½ cup butter
1 *pound cottage cheese*
¼ cup sour cream
1 *cup chopped walnuts*

1 *cup raisins (if you want them)*
Salt to taste
1 *teaspoon cinnamon*
2 *eggs, beaten (optional)*

Cook the noodles in some salted spring water. While they are cooking, mix the butter and cottage cheese with the sour cream, chopped walnuts, raisins, salt, and cinnamon. Now add the beaten eggs, if you want to use them, to the cheese mixture. The eggs act as a binder, and allow you to cut the kugel into squares when you serve it. (I don't use the eggs, so it just comes out sort of mushy, but it still tastes the same and that is the only important thing.) After the cheese mixture is ready, add the noodles to it and stir it up. Pour it all into a buttered square cake dish and sprinkle with some more cinnamon. (The recipe doesn't call for it, but I sprinkle about ¼ cup sesame seeds on top, too, for a little boost.)

Bake at 350° for 30 minutes and serve hot.

BLINTZES

4–6 SERVINGS

EXTERNAL

2 cups milk	2 tablespoons melted butter
2 cups sifted whole-wheat	(careful not to scorch it)
pastry flour	Butter for frying
2 eggs	Sour cream
½ teaspoon salt	Fresh berries in season

Slowly beat the milk into the flour (doing it slowly prevents lumps). Beat the eggs and then add to the flour mixture, beating till smooth. Add the salt and melted butter.

Heat a small frying pan and put in enough butter to cover the bottom of the pan. Pour a thin layer of batter into the pan and brown over low heat. (This is important. You should never use a high heat because it prevents the batter from cooking to a proper consistency.) Brown on both sides, being careful not to scorch. Remove from the pan and keep warm. Repeat until all the batter is used up.

Add 2 tablespoons of the filling mixture (see below) to each external blintz and fold up, tucking in the ends. Place in a greased frying pan and quick fry them to your desired color and texture. (I like crunchy things, so I fry them as long as possible.) You can also bake them in a greased baking dish at about 350° for 15 minutes.

Serve them with sour cream and fresh berries if they are in season.

INTERNAL

2 eggs	*1 tablespoon honey*
1 pound cottage cheese	*½ teaspoon cinnamon*

Beat the eggs and then mix into the cottage cheese. Add the honey and cinnamon and mix well.

Vegetables on the Side

NUTTY BEETS

3–4 SERVINGS

1 *bunch beets, peeled, sliced,*
and cooked
3 *cups spring water*
¼ *cup grated horseradish*
1 *teaspoon honey*

1 *teaspoon salt*
¼ *cup light vegetable oil*
½ *cup cider vinegar*
½ *cup chopped nuts*

Cook the beets in the spring water until tender, about 20 minutes. Drain and save the water. When the sliced beets have cooled, slice them into thin strips. Mix the grated horseradish, honey, salt, oil, and vinegar.

Put the beets and the nuts in a bowl and toss around a bit. Pour the liquid you saved over the nutty beets and chill in the refrigerator for 3 hours.

SWEET AND SOUR BEETS

3–4 SERVINGS

There are usually three beets in a bunch where I buy them, and when they are sliced there is enough for three people, unless you want to make this a main course. Then there is enough for one person.

1 bunch of beets

2 cups boiling, salted spring water

2 tablespoons butter

2 tablespoons flour, approximately (I usually use whole-wheat pastry flour, but any will do)

¼ cup vinegar (I use cider vinegar, but it's up to you)

¼ cup sour cream

1 teaspoon honey

½ teaspoon salt

¼ teaspoon pepper

Cut the tops off from the beets. (Don't throw the beet tops away. You can steam them in a little water with some lemon juice and your favorite spices and have a great treat. If you like spinach this will be a nice treat for you.) Peel the beets with your potato peeler. Slice them about ¼ inch thick and cook them, covered, in 2 cups of boiling, salted spring water for 10 to 15 minutes, or until tender. Remove the beets and set aside, but save the water from the beets.

In a saucepan melt the butter, add the flour, and blend to a pasty consistency. Add ½ cup of beet water and stir. Add the vinegar and stir. Now slowly add the sour cream and keep stirring as you add it. Add the honey, salt, and pepper. Stir well till smooth and creamy. If the sauce is too thick, add a little more of the beet water, and if it is too thin add a little more flour or a little arrowroot starch. When the sauce is satisfactory, add the beets and cook over low heat (simmer) for 5 to 10 minutes.

SWEET AND SOUR CABBAGE

ABOUT 4 SERVINGS

6 cups shredded cabbage (Mix red and green if you

can get them both)

½ cup grated apple

1 *teaspoon salt*	4 *tablespoons cider vinegar*
¾ *cup spring water*	1 *tablespoon honey*
1 *tablespoon whole-wheat flour*	2 *tablespoons butter*
	½ *cup raisins (optional)*

Cook the cabbage with the apple and salt in the water over low heat for 15 minutes.

Mix the flour with the vinegar until smooth. Add to the cabbage, along with the honey and the butter. Add the raisins now if you want them. Cook 15 minutes longer.

I can't begin to tell you how much I love this dish. The last time I made it I sautéed about 1 cup of sliced mushrooms and added them as a surprise. Everyone said, "Goody!"

CABBAGE AND CHEESE

3–4 SERVINGS

1 *head of cabbage*	¾ *cup grated Monterey Jack cheese*
3 *tablespoons butter*	1 *teaspoon caraway seeds*
3 *tablespoons whole-wheat flour or arrowroot starch*	¼ *cup mixed sunflower and sesame seeds*
1½ *cups milk*	

Chop up the cabbage into small chunks. Steam it for about 10 minutes, or boil it your own way. Make a cream sauce by melting the butter in a pan, stirring in the flour with a whisk, adding the milk, and stirring well until the sauce is thickened. When it is ready, remove it from the heat and add the grated cheese and the seeds. Stir the sauce until it becomes smooth and all the cheese is melted. Pour the sauce over the drained cabbage and place it in a buttered baking dish. Bake it for about 15 minutes, or until the cheese begins to brown.

When I make this dish, I sometimes add some sautéed celery along with the cabbage for a little extra. Zucchini in a small proportion is good, too. The important thing to remember is that in most cases, where this would be a side dish for most people, it will be the main course for me and my guests. So it is better to load it up with things, so everyone won't walk away wondering where the base of the meal is.

HONEYED CARROTS

3–4 SERVINGS

3 tablespoons butter
4 cups cooked carrots
3 tablespoons orange or lemon juice
1 ½ teaspoons salt

4 tablespoons honey (I suggest that you select a light-flavored honey for this recipe)

Combine all the ingredients in a saucepan. Cover and cook at a simmer for 20 to 25 minutes, stirring every once in a while. (If you get yourself really set up in the kitchen, you can arrange a system for yourself where everything just gets stirred whenever you happen to pass it on the stove. That is why I love wooden spoons so much. I can put one in each thing I'm preparing, or beside each thing, and whenever I go by the stove I just give a little stir to everything. The wooden spoons never get hot, don't damage the bottoms of your pans, and never alter the taste.)

SNOW PEAS AND NUTS

ABOUT 4 SERVINGS

1 pound snow peas (They are also called "pea pods")
¼ cup sesame seeds

2 tablespoons butter
¼ cup chopped walnuts
Chopped parsley

Steam the snow peas until they are tender, about 20 minutes. While they are steaming, toast the sesame seeds in the butter. After they have been toasting about 3 minutes, add the walnuts and cook them along with the seeds for another 4 minutes, stirring constantly. When the snow peas are tender enough, remove them from the steamer, place them in a vegetable dish, and cover them with the nuts and seeds. Sprinkle a bit of parsley on top and serve.

SESAME SQUASH

4–6 SERVINGS

1 *pound yellow crookneck squash*	*¼ cup sesame seeds*
	½ cup pumpkin seeds
2 *tablespoons butter*	*Juice of ½ lemon*

Wash the squash and slice it into ½-inch-thick pieces. Steam the squash in a Dutch oven over a little water. (I often throw a clove of garlic into the water away from the squash; the garlic steams with the water and some of the flavor is absorbed by the squash.) While the squash are steaming, melt the butter over a low flame and then add the seeds, stirring them constantly as they toast. (Don't freak out when the pumpkin seeds begin to pop like popcorn. It is a real gas to watch them. That is why you should keep the flame low; otherwise they will pop all over the room. If you find that they are doing that, then you will have to cover the pan and keep shaking it as though it was popcorn.)

When the squash are steamed to your desired crispness, then remove them and place them in a bowl. Pour the toasted seeds and the butter over the squash and squeeze the lemon juice over them. Serve immediately.

Vegetables should be prepared when everything else for the meal is practically done. This way they can be served as soon as they are done, and then they will still be warm.

TOMATO ON THE SIDE

8 SERVINGS

8 *ripe tomatoes*
¼ *cup bread or cracker crumbs (I use rye cracker crumbs, similar to Ry-Krisp, and I love what they do)*
1 ½ *teaspoons basil (If you aren't a basil fan, use what you like)*

1 ½ *teaspoons chopped parsley*
¼ *cup chopped onion*
½ *teaspoon garlic salt*
¼ *cup butter, approximately*
8 *small slices cheese*

Cut out the bottom centers of the tomatoes and place them, bottoms up, in a buttered baking dish. If you are starting with whole crackers or bread, put them into the blender and whiz them around for a few seconds. It makes the nicest crumbs, and they look good on food. Mix the crumbs with the basil, parsley, onion and garlic salt. Sprinkle the tomatoes with the mixture, and then put ½ tablespoon butter on each tomato. Bake 10 minutes at 400°, and then remove from the oven. If the tomatoes seem dry, add a little more butter.

Now place a small slice of cheese on top of each tomato and put them under the broiler until the cheese melts and browns a little, about 3 minutes. (The kind of cheese isn't important. I usually just see whatever I have in the refrigerator and then pick out the oldest one and use it.)

BROCCOLI

Broccoli is one of the vegetables that I cook alone and rarely add anything to. I of course steam it, and as soon as it begins to darken in color I know that it is done. I like it when it is nice and chewy. Sometimes I add a little butter and, of course, a few seeds, but rarely unless I am trying to impress someone do I put a cheese or cream sauce on it. It really doesn't need it.

VEGETABLE COMBINATIONS

If I am making a vegetable to use as a side dish, there usually isn't too much that goes into the preparation. I simply clean and cut whatever it is and steam it for however long it takes. Then, when it is ready, I decide if I am going to put roasted seeds on top or maybe a cream or cheese sauce. Certain vegetables make good combinations, like:

GREEN BEANS WITH MUSHROOMS
4–6 SERVINGS

The recipe for mushrooms and peas, given below, can also be made by substituting green beans for the peas. I never cut green beans into tiny pieces, because I think they look prettier whole. I steam them till they are just tender but still crisp and then add the mushrooms. And when I don't feel like the mushrooms, I sliver some almonds and toast them in the butter with the sesame seeds. This makes a nice small side dish to what will be a main dish of vegetables, too. The main idea is to use vegetables in the side dish that haven't been used in the main dish. That is why this is nice, because I can leave the mushrooms out and it can still be very good. (I usually put mushrooms in all my main courses.)

KIDNEY BEANS AND TOMATOES
4–6 SERVINGS

1 *cup dried kidney beans*
Spring water to cover

3 *ripe tomatoes, peeled*
½ *onion, chopped*

1 teaspoon basil   1 teaspoon arrowroot starch,
½ teaspoon salt   approximately

Soak the kidney beans overnight, then drain and rinse them. When you are ready to make the dish, boil the beans in fresh spring water to cover for 15 to 20 minutes. Peel the tomatoes and chop them up into small pieces, along with the onion. Add to the beans and stir everything. Add the basil, salt, and starch and stir till the sauce thickens. Add more starch, if necessary. Serve hot.

MUSHROOMS AND FRESH PEAS
4–6 SERVINGS

1 ½ cups shelled fresh peas   1 ¼ tablespoons butter
2 cups fresh, sliced mush-   Sesame seeds (optional)
rooms   Lemon juice (optional)

Steam or boil the peas until they are tender. While they are cooking, sauté the mushrooms in the butter, with some sesame seeds if you like, and when both peas and mushrooms are done mix them together and serve. Squeeze a little lemon juice on top for zing, if you like.

SPINACH AND TOMATOES
4–6 SERVINGS

1 clove garlic   ¼ cup chopped onion
1 pound spinach   ½ teaspoon orégano
3 tablespoons olive oil   Sprouts or seeds for garnish
4 ripe tomatoes, peeled

Place the clove of garlic in the water that you are going to steam the spinach in before you put the leaves into the steamer. Then steam the spinach until the leaves begin to wilt. When the leaves are covered with drops of water you know that they are done. Now heat the olive oil in a saucepan. Add the tomatoes, which you have chopped up a bit, and the onion, and stir them in the oil. Crush that clove of garlic from the steamer water and add it, along with the orégano, to the tomatoes and oil. Now add the spinach and a tiny bit of the steamed water and toss everything up. When it is warm enough, serve it with a few sprouts or seeds sprinkled on top.

Spinach is also good plain, with a few toasted sesame seeds or almonds sprinkled on top.

MUSHROOM TREATS

4–6 SERVINGS

DOUGH

½ pound cream cheese
½ cup softened butter

1 ½ cups sifted whole-wheat
   pastry flour

FILLING

1 onion, finely chopped
3 tablespoons melted butter
½ pound mushrooms,
   chopped
¼ teaspoon thyme

½ teaspoon salt
¼ teaspoon pepper
¼ teaspoon garlic powder
2 tablespoons flour
¼ cup sour cream

To make the dough, blend the cream cheese with the butter. Try using a fork, as if you were making a pie crust. Then add the flour and work the ingredients together with your fingers until smooth. Chill for about 30 minutes.

For the filling, sauté the onion lightly in the butter. Add the mushrooms and sauté them, too, stirring frequently. Add the thyme, salt, pepper, and garlic powder and mix in. Sprinkle the flour over the vegetable mixture and stir in the sour cream. Simmer until it thickens, stirring frequently.

Remove the dough from the refrigerator and roll it out on a floured bread board to about a ⅛-inch thickness. (Thin!) Cut into circles as big as you like. (I use a lid from a jar about 3 inches in diameter.) Place a spoonful of filling in the center of the dough and fold over, sealing the edges with a fork. Place on a ungreased cookie sheet and bake at 450° for 15 minutes, or until brown.

Main Dishes

The following are some of the main-course dishes I have gathered up. There is one ingredient that can and should be put into each one of them. It is natural brewer's yeast. I try and take it every morning, but I just can't stand the taste. So I put it into all my dishes that can camouflage it with their own great taste. Another thing that will lose its taste in most of my casseroles in this section is wheat-germ oil. It is expensive, but all you need to put in is a teaspoon or two and presto, everyone will have a natural vitamin E boost.

I don't consider any of my dishes totally complete. Just what do I mean by that? Well, I mean that I'm sure that, in your own special way, each and every one of you can add your own special touch to almost every one of these recipes and give them all a certain personal flair. Good luck, and good eating!

CREAMED VEGETABLES

4–6 SERVINGS

Asparagus	*Turnips*
Green beans	*Carrots*
Cabbage	*Squash*
Celery	*Zucchini*

Onions   Peas
Mushrooms   Spinach
Swiss chard (red or white)   Green peppers
Beets

These are just some of the vegetables that can go into this dish. The object is to take a selection of fresh vegetables that are in season and combine them. Thus, depending on what time of year you make this dish, you will always have something a little different. I always use onions, almost always carrots, and the only time I would ever consider leaving mushrooms out would be if they were very bad, or if the store was just out of them.

Decide which vegetables you are going to use. You don't need more than 1½ to 2 cups of any one vegetable. Once you have tried the recipe, you can then determine which you want to use more of than others. Always cook to please yourself or whoever you are cooking for and you can never go wrong. Most of my friends love mushrooms, so I always go very heavy on them, no matter what the price happens to be. This always pleases them and thus it pleases me. I have a certain friend who loves peas and radishes, so whenever he eats at my place I make it a point to have them around.

Chop or slice your vegetables whatever way you like. It is nice to vary the shapes of the different vegetables. Never cut them too thick, though (about ¼ inch thick is right), because it will foul up your cooking process. Pay attention to your vegetable charts and note which vegetables take longer than others to cook. Those are the ones you want to make sure aren't cut too thick.

Now you want to steam the vegetables. If you have a steamer then you know what to do. (Unfortunately, as I have said, I have never been able to afford one, so I use my stainless-steel Dutch oven with a stainless-steel vegetable basket standing up in it.) Put just enough water in the bottom of the pan so that it doesn't touch the basket. Bring the water to a boil and leave a medium flame under the pan. Now put the vegetables in the basket to steam. Longest-cooking vegetables go in first, like carrots, turnips, beets, etc. Now, as you notice them begin to soften, put in more of your vegetables until they are all in the basket. Make sure that there is enough water in the pan. (It does evaporate due to the fact that you keep taking the lid off to add vegetables.) It isn't a great problem to keep checking the water, and, besides, it's well worth it because this dish is so good. When you have all the vegetables in the basket, put the lid on the pan and cook them for about 20 minutes, or until they are tender enough for you. I like them when they are still a bit crisp.

In a separate saucepan make a cream sauce:

2 tablespoons butter
2 tablespoons whole-wheat flour or arrowroot starch
1 cup milk
1 teaspoon salt
¼ teaspoon pepper
½ teaspoon chopped parsley
(You can add any other of your favorite herbs and spices for variety. Adding 1 teaspoon curry powder can make a light curry dish that's nice. A combination of 1 teaspoon mustard powder, ½ teaspoon marjoram, and ¼ teaspoon tarragon might also please you)

Put the butter in the pan and melt it. Add the flour and blend the two together. Add the milk and stir constantly with a wire whisk until the sauce begins to thicken. Add the salt, pepper, parsley, and the other herbs and spices you decided on and stir into the cream sauce. Cook over low heat for 10 minutes. Place the vegetables in a serving dish and pour the sauce over them. Mix well and serve.

SELF-STEAMED VEGETABLES

4–6 SERVINGS

This is another method of steaming vegetables that requires a little closer watch on the pot. You should use a flame trivet for sure if you decide to use this method.

You choose the combination of vegetables that you want to use, depending on what is in season and what your preferences are. Here is an example:

Carrots	*Green peppers*
Celery	*Snow peas or fresh peas*
Onions	*Turnips*
Mushrooms	*Cabbage*

This will make a nice combination. But don't limit yourself to this idea. I always wait until I get to the store and see what is in stock. Then I buy a little of everything that looks good and then it practically puts itself together. The only planning ahead that is required for this dish is making your mind up that this is the one you are going to make. Once you get to the store you may find something that I haven't even mentioned staring you in the face saying, "Wouldn't I be good in your dinner tonight?" And you would have to agree, "Yes." So you take it and throw it in and the dish may take on a whole new flavor.

If you don't have a steamer, use a stainless-steel Dutch oven. Place 3 tablespoons cold-pressed cooking oil in your pan and let it heat for a minute over a low fire. Now add your vegetables, one kind at a time, carefully placing the ones that take the longest time to cook in first. Remember, the harder they are the longer they take. Thus carrots, turnips, and celery would definitely go in before the mushrooms and the onions. Cover and cook them over a low heat. As you add each vegetable be sure to turn it over with a wooden spoon in the oil, so it will absorb some of the oil, too. Watch them carefully, and when they are tender enough for you then they are ready. As I said before, I like them crisp, so I don't cook my vegetables too long.

These vegetables are ready to eat when you remove them from the pan. You may just want to salt them a bit. However, if you want to make a sauce for them, try a light curry sauce by following these directions:

In a saucepan melt 3 tablespoons butter. Add 3 tablespoons arrowroot starch and blend with the butter. Add 1 cup of milk and stir the mixture well. Add about 1 teaspoon curry powder and stir it in carefully, watching so that the sauce doesn't get too thick. (Always cook cream sauces over a low flame and use a flame trivet if you have one. They are quite valuable in times like these.) Add a little salt and pepper, and taste the sauce. If you like a stronger flavor you may want to add more curry. I like mine very light, so you will have to work around that. Add a little chopped parsley, too, if you like it. It doesn't necessarily go with the curry, but I add it anyway.

CHOW YENTA

ABOUT 4 SERVINGS

Light vegetable oil	1 cup cubed Tofu (page 58; optional)
3 cups sliced celery (sliced thinly, on the diagonal)	1 cup spring water
2 cups sliced onions	1/3 cup soy sauce
3 cups fresh bean sprouts	1 tablespoon arrowroot starch
3–4 cups sliced mushrooms	1 teaspoon honey (optional)
1/4 cup parsley, chopped	
1 cup young snow peas	

Put a little oil in your wok and add a sprinkle of water. Cook the vegetables in the wok until they are tender but still crisp (about 15 minutes). While the vegetables are cooking, mix the spring water, soy sauce, and arrowroot starch together until the starch is well blended. You can add 1 teaspoon of honey to the mixture if you think you might want it here. (I don't usually do it myself.) Pour the sauce over the vegetables, add Tofu and heat for a few minutes, until the sauce bubbles a bit. Serve with rice if you want to. This is a dish that I find to be satisfying enough without the rice, and I think it is good to have a few meals that are totally free of starch, so I just serve it with a salad.

YENTA SUEY

ABOUT 4 SERVINGS

1 *large onion, cut up*
1½ *cups sliced celery*
2–3 *cups sliced mushrooms*
Light vegetable oil
4 *cups bean sprouts (Re-member, you can make* *them yourself [page 19]. It sure does make a differ-ence, just wait and see!)*
1 *teaspoon honey*
1 *cup soy sauce*

Cook the onion, celery, and mushrooms in your wok with a little oil, or in your steamer until they are tender but still crisp. Whatever you do, try not to let them get soft or soggy. Crisp, crisp, crisp. When they are ready, add the sprouts and cook for a few minutes. Now add the honey and the soy sauce. Heat just long enough for the soy sauce to get hot. Serve over some fresh-cooked brown rice.

VEGETABLE ROAST

ABOUT 4 SERVINGS

1 *cup sliced onions*
½ *cup butter or light vege-table oil*
2 *cups string beans, cut up in small slices*
1 *cup chopped celery*
1 *cup sliced zucchini*
1 *cup shelled peas*
2 *carrots, cut up in chunks*
1 *cup diced turnips*
1 *cup diced potatoes*
1 *cup bread crumbs*
1 *teaspoon salt*
¼ *teaspoon pepper*
1 *teaspoon basil*
1 *tablespoon chopped parsley*

Brown the onions in a little of the butter or oil, whichever you use. (I know that the oil is better for you, but I must confess that I am known to use the butter more often than the oil. The plain truth is that I like the taste that the butter gives more than the taste of the oil. I know, shame on me. But no one can do everything perfectly all the time. One of my weaknesses is butter, and I am sure that it will catch up with me sooner or later. If you can, use the oil, it definitely is better for you.) Place the onions in a deep casserole that has a lid. Now combine the bread crumbs with the remaining butter, salt, pepper, and basil until they are evenly mixed. I use my hand and just squish them together until the butter is completely taken in by the bread crumbs. Place layers of the vegetables in the casserole, alternating with bread crumbs and a sprinkle of the parsley until they are all in the casserole. Bake at 400° for 20 minutes.

Now remove the casserole from the oven and turn it down to 350°. Take off the lid and stir the vegetables up so that the ones on top can go down to the bottom and absorb some of the juices. Return the covered casserole dish to the lowered oven and bake for 1 hour.

When you plan this dish, don't limit yourself to just the vegetables that I have suggested. Do the planning when you are at the store in front of the vegetable section, when you can see what looks good and what is going at a good price. I always wait until I can see just what is going on before I make any final decisions. One good thing about doing it this way is that nothing comes out exactly the same every time unless it is a dish that I want to be the same every time, like Mushrooms with Sour Cream (page 91). (That is so good, I wouldn't change a thing in it except for maybe a little extra dry mustard every once in a while.)

CARROT CASSEROLE

4–6 SERVINGS

1½ cups raw brown rice
3 cups spring water
Salt
1 onion, chopped
1 tablespoon butter
1 cup bread or cracker
  crumbs
½ teaspoon basil
4 cups grated carrots

½ cup chopped walnuts
  (This is optional, but I
  can't imagine leaving the
  nuts out)
½ cup raisins (optional)
1 tablespoon wheat-germ oil
  (optional)

Cook the rice in the 3 cups of spring water with a sprinkle of salt. While the rice is cooking, sauté the onion in the butter. (You can also use a light vegetable oil in place of the butter. I just happen to be a real freak for the flavor that I get from sautéeing my vegetables in butter.) When the onions are just about done (don't let them brown), add the bread crumbs and the basil and stir a little till they sort of toast a bit. Now grate the carrots, by which time your rice should be almost done. Add the bread-crumb mixture and the carrots to the rice in a bowl and mix well. Now add the nuts and the raisins. It is a good idea to add about 1 tablespoon of wheat-germ oil here, too, and then mix everything up good. Put the mixture in a casserole and bake it at 350° for about 1 hour.

BAKED CAULIFLOWER

2–3 SERVINGS

1 whole cauliflower
½ cup rye cracker crumbs
¼ cup sesame seeds or sunflower seeds
2 tablespoons butter
2 tablespoons arrowroot

starch or whole-wheat
flour
1 cup milk
½ cup grated cheese (Mon-
  terey Jack or Swiss)
1 teaspoon chopped parsley

Steam the whole cauliflower until it is tender, about 30 minutes. Remove it, place it in a deep casserole dish, and cover it with the cracker crumbs and the seeds. Make a sauce by melting the butter and adding the starch or flour, stirring with a wire whisk until a paste forms. Now add the milk and simmer, stirring constantly with the whisk, until the sauce thickens. When it begins to thicken, add the grated cheese and the parsley and stir. Pour the sauce over the cauliflower and bake it in the oven at 350° for about 15 minutes.

CUCUMBERS, MUSHROOMS, AND CHEESE

3–4 SERVINGS

½ pound mushrooms
¼ cup chopped onion
¼ cup butter
1 large cucumber
2 tablespoons whole-wheat flour or arrowroot starch
1½ cups milk
1 cup grated Swiss cheese or mild Cheddar (I prefer the Swiss and sometimes I add some Monterey Jack to the Swiss, but you can use whatever you prefer here.

I personally don't think sharp Cheddar with its distinct taste does anything for the dish)
½ teaspoon salt
Pinch of pepper (If you are using a pepper grinder, I consider 2 twists of the grinder to be about the same as a pinch)
¼ cup sunflower seeds
½ cup rye cracker crumbs

Clean and slice the mushrooms and sauté them, along with the onions, in 2 tablespoons of the butter. Peel and slice the cucumber. (You can use the skin if you want, but I find that cucumber skin is too bitter for my taste buds, so I remove it.)

Make a cheese sauce by melting the remaining butter in a saucepan and adding the flour, stirring to a paste with a wire whisk. Now add the milk and stir constantly until the sauce begins to thicken.

When it does begin to thicken, remove it from the flame and add the grated cheese, salt, and pepper. (I add about 2 teaspoons of chopped parsley here because I just can't seem to keep parsley out of anything.) Stir the sauce until the cheese is melted and smooth. Now stir in the cucumbers and the other vegetables. When they are covered evenly with the sauce, stir in the sunflower seeds and most of the cracker crumbs. Pour into a buttered casserole dish and sprinkle the top with the rest of the cracker crumbs. Bake at 350° for 20 minutes, or until the cheese begins to brown.

WEIRD EGGPLANT

ABOUT 3 SERVINGS

This is for those people who hate eggplant. Like me! It's so moist and crunchy they won't believe it's eggplant. People who like eggplant will recognize it and like it, too.

1 *eggplant*	2 *cups grated cheese (I use*
2 *egg yolks, beaten*	*Monterey Jack and mild*
Juice of 1 lemon	*Cheddar both, but you can*
1 *teaspoon salt*	*use any cheese that you*
½ *teaspoon pepper*	*may prefer)*

Peel the eggplant, cut it in 1-inch slices, and soak in cold water for 1 hour. Drain and dry.

Mix the egg yolks with the lemon juice, salt, and pepper. Place a few slices in a buttered casserole dish and brush with the egg and lemon mixture. Then sprinkle with some of the cheese. Repeat until all the eggplant is in the casserole. Put the remaining cheese on top and pour over the remaining liquid. Bake at 350° for about 40 minutes.

EGGPLANT BURGERS

ABOUT 3 SERVINGS

1 eggplant
¼ cup chopped onion
½ teaspoon salt
2 tablespoons soy sauce

¼ cup cornmeal
1 cup whole-wheat bread crumbs
¼ cup ground almonds

Bake the whole eggplant in the oven for about 1½ hours at about 325°. When you remove it from the oven let it cool, and then peel it. Put it into the blender and let it whiz around until it becomes an even consistency. Don't let it go too long, or it will get too liquidy. Remove it from the blender and put it into a bowl. Add the rest of the ingredients and mix them all well. (If you don't have bread crumbs around, all you have to do is slice enough bread and put it into the oven for a few minutes until it dries out. Then put it into the blender and whiz it until presto, you have bread crumbs. I sometimes make this recipe with half whole-wheat and half rye cracker or bread crumbs.) When all the ingredients are mixed together well, form into patties and place on a greased cookie sheet and bake at 350° for about 30 minutes. You can also broil them but you've got to watch them closely. (Also you can fry them, but that is a bit fattening, you know.) Serve with a little cheese and a big handful of sprouts on the side.

EGGPLANT-TOMATO DINNER

4–6 SERVINGS

2 eggplants, peeled and diced
3 tablespoons butter
4 tomatoes, sliced
1 teaspoon salt
¼ teaspoon pepper

¼ cup chopped parsley
1 teaspoon basil
1½ cups rye cracker crumbs or bread crumbs, if you prefer

¼ cup grated Parmesan   ¼ cup grated Monterey Jack
cheese   cheese

Sauté the eggplant chunks in the butter until they become a bit tender. Then place in a buttered casserole and cover with the sliced tomatoes. Mix the salt, pepper, parsley, and basil with the cracker crumbs and sprinkle over the tomatoes and eggplant. Sprinkle with the grated cheese and then bake at 350° for about 45 minutes, or until the cheese begins to brown.

MUSHROOMS WITH SOUR CREAM

ABOUT 4 SERVINGS

1 cup diced onions   ¾ teaspoon salt
5 tablespoons butter   1 teaspoon paprika
1 ½ pounds mushrooms,   ¼ teaspoon dry mustard
    sliced   1 cup sour cream
¼ teaspoon pepper

Sauté the onions in half the butter and set aside. Add the remaining butter to the sauté pan and sauté the mushrooms. Return onions to the pan and add the spices. Cook 5 minutes over low heat. Add the sour cream and serve over whole-wheat noodles.

This is one of my very favorite dishes. It is just like beef Stroganoff, only without the beef and there is no wine in this dish. I like serving this dish with Sweet and Sour Cabbage (page 71) because the two juices are good when they run together.

SCALLOPED MUSHROOMS

2 SERVINGS

2 dozen large mushrooms   rye crackers)
¾ cup cracker crumbs (I use   ¼ teaspoon paprika

¼ teaspoon orégano
½ teaspoon salt
¼ teaspoon garlic salt
2 tablespoons softened butter

¾ cup chopped celery
¼ cup chopped parsley
1 cup cream

Clean the mushrooms. Grease a small casserole dish. Combine the cracker crumbs, paprika, orégano, salt, and garlic salt and give it all a quick whiz in the blender. Pour into a bowl and add the butter, squishing it around with your hands until the crackers are blended with the butter.

Place a layer of mushrooms in the buttered casserole dish. Now place a layer of the chopped celery over the mushrooms, then a layer of the cracker crumbs. Sprinkle with some parsley. Repeat the layering, starting with the mushrooms, until everything is in the casserole dish except for a little of the crumb mixture. Pour the cream over the mushrooms and sprinkle the remaining crumbs on top. Bake at 350° for about 25 minutes.

MUSHROOMS IN SESAME-SEED SAUCE

ABOUT 4 SERVINGS

12 small white onions
1½ cups shelled peas
½ cup sesame seeds
¼ cup sesame oil (You can substitute your favorite vegetable oil here, if you want a lighter flavor. Sesame oil is very strong, especially unrefined)

2 cups thinly sliced green onions (This usually takes two to three bunches; use all the onion and greens)
½ cup soy sauce
1 tablespoon honey
1 clove garlic, minced
2 pounds mushrooms

Peel the onions and place them in boiling water for 3 to 5 minutes. Remove them from the water carefully, trying not to let them separate. Now put the peas in the same water and boil them for 5 to 7 minutes. Remove them and set aside with the onions. (I don't cook the peas till they are soft because I like them when they are as close to raw as possible. Thus you may have to cook them another 5 minutes if you want them tender.)

Brown the sesame seeds in 1 tablespoon of the oil. Mix the seeds, green onions, soy sauce, honey, garlic, and half the remaining oil in a bowl. Clean and slice the mushrooms into ½-inch slices. Place the sliced mushrooms in the sesame-seed mixture and marinate for about 1 hour.

Remove the mushrooms from the sauce and sauté them in the remaining oil. Add the marinade, white onions, and peas and bring to a boil. Reduce the heat to low and cook for 10 minutes. Serve hot, over brown rice.

ALMOND-MUSHROOM CHOP SUEY

ABOUT 3 SERVINGS

Light vegetable oil
1 large onion, cut up
1 cup chopped celery
1 cup cut up green pepper
3-4 cups sliced mushrooms
1½ cups sliced or chopped almonds

1 cup spring water
⅓ cup soy sauce
1 tablespoon arrowroot starch
1 teaspoon honey (optional)

In your wok, place a little oil and a sprinkle of water and cook the vegetables until they are tender, making sure that they are still crisp. When they are done, add the almonds and make a sauce by combining the spring water, soy sauce, arrowroot starch, and honey. Pour the sauce over the cooked vegetables and heat until the sauce begins to bubble. Serve hot.

GREEN PEPPER–MUSHROOM SUEY

ABOUT 4 SERVINGS

This is my friend Sharron's recipe. She uses steak in it and thus calls it Mushroom–Green Pepper Beef, which is a popular number in many Chinese restaurants, but I am of course leaving out the beef because who needs it? Sharron does, and we often have words about our differences, but we still are friends even though we seldom eat together any more. I think that she is stubborn, and she thinks that I am a fool. Sounds like a weird relationship, doesn't it? Well, this is nothing compared to some of my other relationships. I guess you might say that I like controversy in my life. Yes, you definitely would say that about me.

1 *onion*	1 *teaspoon honey (optional)*
¾ *pound mushrooms*	1 *tablespoon arrowroot starch*
2 *green peppers*	1 ½ *cups snow peas*
3 *stalks Swiss chard*	2 *cups fresh bean sprouts*
2 *tablespoons butter or oil*	4 *cups cooked Correct Brown*
1 ½–2 *cups soy sauce*	*Rice (page 47)*

Cut up the different vegetables in whatever way you think will look nice. (I do it differently each time. One suggestion is not to make any pieces too small.) Sauté the onion, mushrooms, peppers, and Swiss chard in the butter or oil (whichever you choose), and while they are cooking mix the soy sauce with the honey and the starch. Now add the sauce to the vegetables and stir. Add the snow peas and simmer the dish for ten minutes. Add the bean sprouts and let them get warm. Don't cook the dish any longer than it takes for the sprouts to get warm, though, because then the vegetables will get too soft.

Serve the dish over brown rice that you should have had cooking while you were preparing the dish.

STUFFED GREEN PEPPERS

4–6 SERVINGS

½ pound mushrooms, sliced
5 tablespoons butter
2 cups chopped onion
2 cups cooked brown rice
2 teaspoons salt
½ teaspoon pepper

1 ½ tablespoons wheat-germ oil
½ cup chopped walnuts
¼ cup sunflower seeds
6 green peppers
6 slices cheese (optional)

Sauté the mushrooms in half the butter. Remove and set aside. Sauté the onion in the remaining butter. In a large mixing bowl combine the sautéed vegetables with the rice, salt, pepper, and wheat-germ oil. Mix well. (Depending on the season, I use other vegetables in this dish. If squash is cheap I will sauté some and put it in, too. Sometimes I add fresh peas around July and August when they are in season. Use your favorite, whatever it may be, and then you will have a special dish suited to your own taste.) Add the nuts and seeds and mix again.

Now cut off the tops of the green peppers and clean them out with a well-rounded spoon so the peppers won't get punctured. Stuff each pepper and place in a casserole dish. When each is stuffed, place the remaining rice mixture in the dish around the peppers. If you like, place a slice of your favorite cheese on top of each pepper and place the tops on the peppers. More cheese can be placed on the rice in the dish, too, if you want. (I put lots on because I like it.) Bake at 350° for about 25 minutes, or until the peppers look soft.

COTTAGE-CHEESE STUFFED PEPPERS

3–4 SERVINGS

1 onion, chopped
1 cup sliced mushrooms

2 tablespoons wheat-germ oil
1 pound cottage cheese

2 *cups cooked brown rice*
1 *teaspoon salt*
2 *teaspoons chopped parsley*
¼ *teaspoon pepper*
1 *teaspoon basil*

2 *ripe tomatoes*
4 *large green peppers*
Sunflower seeds
Sesame seeds

Sauté the onion and the mushrooms in the wheat-germ oil, and then add them to the cottage cheese. Mix well and add the cooked rice and the herbs and spices. Stir everything together, then chop up the tomatoes and add them.

Slice off the lids of the peppers and clean them out with a small wooden spoon, which will help to prevent puncturing of the peppers. Place the cleaned peppers in a baking dish and stuff each one with the cheese mixture. Place whatever is left over around the peppers in the dish. Sprinkle everything with lots of sunflower seeds and sesame seeds and replace the lids on the peppers. Bake at 350° for about 25 minutes, or until the peppers look nice and soft.

POTATO PANCAKES

3–4 SERVINGS

4 *potatoes*
2 *tablespoons butter*
1 *cup milk*
¼ *cup grated onion*
½ *teaspoon salt*

Pinch of pepper
¼ *cup sunflower seeds*
1 *egg, beaten*
Melted butter or oil for frying

Boil the potatoes until they are tender. Remove them from the heat and run cool water over them until they are cool enough for you to handle and peel. After you have peeled the potatoes, mash them with the butter and milk. (I usually whip them with my hand mixer for a few minutes while I add the milk.)

When the potatoes are ready, add the rest of the ingredients and mix together well. Now fry small amounts in the melted butter or oil until they are brown on one side, then turn and brown them on the second side.

This is one of the few things that I eat with eggs, even though I try and keep them out of my diet. Potato pancakes are just one of those things from my past that I can't leave behind. So every once in a while I sneak a few in just for nostalgia.

POTATO CASSEROLE

2 SERVINGS

1 *large white potato, thinly sliced*
1 *cup dried spinach noodles*
1 *onion, chopped*
¼ *pound mushrooms (You can use less if you want. I love mushrooms, so I tend to use a lot in everything I make)*

2 *tablespoons butter*
¾ *cup milk*
1½ *tablespoons whole-wheat flour*
½ *teaspoon salt*
⅛ *teaspoon pepper*
½ *teaspoon lemon juice*
⅓ *cup sliced almonds*
½ *cup sour cream*

Boil the potato until the slices are just barely tender. Boil the noodles till tender, too. (Don't forget to salt the water before putting the noodles in the water. Another good thing to do is to rinse the noodles before you put them in the water; it helps to eliminate some of the starch before cooking. Always rinse the noodles *after* cooking.)

Sauté the onion and the mushrooms in the butter. Make a white sauce (page 82) in your double boiler, if you have one. Pour the milk into the top of the double boiler, add the flour, and stir. Then add the salt, pepper, and lemon juice and continue to stir until the sauce thickens. Add the mushrooms, onions, and almonds.

Add the noodles, potatoes, and sour cream to the white sauce. Stir a little and put it into a casserole dish. Bake at 450° for 15 to 20 minutes.

POTATO KUGEL

4–6 SERVINGS

4 eggs, beaten
2 teaspoons salt
1 teaspoon baking powder
Dash of pepper
8 large potatoes, peeled, grated, and drained (I use white potatoes)

½ cup softened butter
¾ cup chopped nuts (Sunflower seeds are also good here)
½ cup raisins (if you want)

Add the eggs, salt, baking powder, and pepper to the potatoes and mix it up well. Melt the butter and put enough into the baking dish to grease it well. Add the remaining butter to the potato mixture and add the nuts and raisins, if you need them. (I guess I shouldn't be so hard on raisins; they do have iron in them, so I guess they can't be all bad.) Mix well, pour into the baking dish, and bake at 400° for 45 minutes.

POTATO-CURRY CASSEROLE

2–3 SERVINGS

1 ¼ cups mashed potatoes
6 tablespoons butter
1 onion, chopped
1 ½ cups sliced mushrooms
⅓ cup whole-wheat pastry flour
1 cup cottage cheese

1 ½ teaspoons salt
¼ teaspoon pepper
¼ cup chopped parsley
½ cup sunflower seeds or pumpkin seeds
½ cup milk
½–1 teaspoon curry powder

If you don't have leftover potatoes, then you have to make them first before you start the dish. It takes about 3 or 4 potatoes (depending on the size) to make 1¼ cups of mashed potatoes. After you have them made, melt 4 tablespoons of the butter in a skillet and sauté the onion and the mushrooms in it. Add the flour and stir it until the mixture forms a pasty consistency. Now add the cottage cheese, 1 teaspoon of the salt, and the pepper, along with the parsley and seeds, and stir well.

In a saucepan combine the milk with the rest of the salt and the remaining 2 tablespoons butter. Bring to a boil and remove from the heat right away. Add the curry powder and then beat in the potatoes. Put the vegetables into a buttered casserole and pour the potatoes over them. Place in the oven at 350° for 20 minutes and then under the broiler for 5 minutes, or until the potatoes brown. Serve hot.

SPINACH-MUSHROOM CASSEROLE

ABOUT 3 SERVINGS

2 cups sliced mushrooms	4 cups cooked spinach
4 tablespoons butter	½ cup grated Cheddar cheese
2 tablespoons whole-wheat flour	½ teaspoon salt
1 cup milk	¼ teaspoon pepper
	½ cup chopped walnuts

Sauté the mushrooms in 2 tablespoons of the butter and then make a cheese sauce by melting the remaining butter, stirring in the flour with a whisk, and adding the milk, stirring constantly with the whisk. When it begins to thicken, add the grated cheese and stir until smooth. When the sauce is smooth and creamy, add the spinach and the mushrooms, along with the salt, pepper, and chopped walnuts, and put it all into a baking dish. Bake at 325° for 20 minutes and serve as soon as it is ready.

SAUERKRAUT AND RICE

3–4 SERVINGS

2 cups cooked brown rice
1 large onion, chopped
1 large green pepper, chopped
3 tablespoons butter

2 cups sauerkraut
¼ cup chopped parsley
Dry mustard (optional)
Sunflower seeds

Have the rice ready, and then sauté the onion and the green pepper in the butter. Mix the vegetables with the sauerkraut and then mix in the rice. Add the parsley and a little dry mustard, if you like. Heat for about 10 minutes over low heat and serve hot, with some sunflower seeds on top.

TOMATO-LENTIL CASSEROLE

4 SERVINGS

1 pound lentils
1 tablespoon soy sauce
1 clove garlic, minced
½ cup chopped onions
½ cup chopped celery
2 tablespoons light vegetable oil

1 cup rye cracker crumbs
1 teaspoon salt
1 teaspoon thyme
2 cups tomatoes

Cook the lentils with the soy sauce. While they are cooking, sauté the garlic, onions, and celery in some of the oil. When they are tender, remove from the flame and mix with the cracker crumbs, salt, and thyme. Add to the cooked lentils, along with the tomatoes and the rest of the oil. Mix well, put into a casserole dish, and bake for about 45 minutes at 350°.

TOMATO-ZUCCHINI CASSEROLE

ABOUT 4 SERVINGS

1 onion, chopped
½ cup chopped celery
2 tablespoons butter
1 pound fresh zucchini, sliced
3–4 fresh, very ripe tomatoes
½ teaspoon salt
¼ teaspoon pepper

½ teaspoon basil
½ cup sunflower seeds
¾ cup grated cheese (I prefer to use Monterey Jack, but it really doesn't matter)
½ cup fresh bean sprouts

Sauté the onion and the celery in the butter. Add the zucchini and let it cook for about 5 minutes. (You don't want to let it cook too long, because it will get too soft. If you only cook it 3 minutes it will be just as good, but no more than 5.) Add the tomatoes now, and sort of break them up a bit. Add the salt, pepper, and basil, along with the seeds. Place it all in a buttered casserole dish and cover it with the cheese. Bake at 350° for 20 minutes, or until the cheese turns brown. Serve hot, with the sprouts as a garnish.

ZUCCHINI AND MUSHROOMS IN CHEESE

ABOUT 4 SERVINGS

1 onion, chopped
1 green pepper, chopped
1½ pounds mushrooms, sliced
1 pound zucchini, cut up
½ cup butter
3 tablespoons whole-wheat flour or arrowroot starch

1½ cups cream
¼ cup chopped parsley
1 cup grated Muenster cheese
Salt (optional)
Basil (optional)
¼ cup sunflower seeds
1 cup rye cracker crumbs

Sauté the onion, green pepper, mushrooms, and the zucchini in 3 tablespoons of the butter until they are tender. Make a cream sauce by melting 3 tablespoons of the butter, stirring in the flour and then the cream, and cooking it over a low flame, stirring constantly, until it begins to thicken. (I always use a wire whisk, if I can find one, because it seems to help everything blend together better.) Add the parsley and the cheese to the sauce and stir until the cheese melts. Add a little salt, if you want to, and maybe a little basil, too. (I do and I don't, depending on my mood.) Now stir the seeds into the sauce.

Combine the cracker crumbs with the rest of the butter and then put the vegetables into a baking dish, layered with the buttered crumbs. When all the vegetables and crumbs are in the dish, pour the cheese sauce over it and bake at 375° for 25 minutes.

PIZZA

ONE, 12-INCH PIZZA

I don't know too many people who don't like pizza. It is one of my favorite things to eat. Whenever I am in New York City, I have a habit of making it my whole diet. I love the "street pizza," as I call it, that you can get on just about every street corner in that city. Here in San Francisco it is a little harder to find, so I just make my own when I want a pizza treat. I am sure that the ingredients that I use are a little purer than those in the pizza in New York, so I hope that you will give it a try. It is a good thing that I don't live in New York, because I would always be cheating by eating the "street pizza."

2 *cups whole-wheat pastry flour*
Olive oil
1 *teaspoon salt*
¼ *cup spring water*
Tomato sauce
Orégano

Cheese (mozzarella or Monterey Jack)
Fresh vegetables
Salt
Basil
Freshly ground pepper

Sift the flour and the salt together. Mix ½ cup olive oil with the water and then pour it over the flour mixture. Cut it with a pastry cutter until the dough can be formed into a ball. You have to make sure that the liquid is evenly distributed throughout the flour mixture. Now roll the dough out as thin as you want it. (I make mine thick, about ½ inch, but if you like it thinner it is up to you.) Place the dough on a greased pan and press it into shape. (If you don't have a pizza pan, which, by the way, are hard to find made out of stainless steel, then you can use a cookie sheet. Just make sure that it has sides on it. I use a square pan for variety, or 2 9-inch Pyrex cake pans.)

Make some tomato sauce (page 20), or else, if you are into canned goods, then you can just use that. Take some olive oil and brush it over the surface of your rolled-out dough. Now spread some tomato sauce over the surface of the dough. Cover it pretty well, but don't use too much because it will get soggy. (One way to prevent it from getting soggy is to put it into a low oven, about 225°, right after you brush on the olive oil, and let it bake for 10 minutes.) After the tomato sauce is on, sprinkle it with orégano. Grate up some mozzarella cheese or Monterey Jack, depending on what is available. Sprinkle a little of it on the pizza, and then spread some fresh-cut vegetables on it. I use mushrooms, onions, and green peppers all the time. Then I vary some zucchini or anchovies. (I have to admit that I always wish that I have a little peperoni lying around in the refrigerator whenever I make this pizza.) Now sprinkle some salt, basil, some more orégano, and some freshly ground pepper over the pie. Now I place slices of fresh tomato on top, too, if I have any extra, and then add the rest of the grated cheese. In all I guess that I use 4 to 5 ounces of cheese per pizza. Sometimes more, depending on my mood.

Bake it at 400° for about 15 minutes.

SALMON PATTIES

ABOUT 4 SERVINGS

This was another favorite summer dinner of mine when I was a kid. The only difference was that we used canned salmon instead of fresh salmon. If you use canned, then you have half the work done for you, but I don't suggest it. I go to a good fish market where I am sure I am at least getting the best fish available. This is, of course, in Chinatown. Here in San Francisco there will be no problem in getting good fresh fish as long as there is a Chinatown. The vegetables, although they may not be organic, are beautiful, too, and I often buy some there if they are not available at my local health food store. I get small salmon steaks (about 1½ pounds) and broil them for about 10 minutes. Then I remove them and flake the meat out and throw away the skin. I place the flaked salmon into a bowl and add 1 chopped onion and 2 tablespoons cider vinegar. My mother used matzoh meal, but I use 1 to 1½ cups powdered sunflower seeds that I grind up in the blender. I then add about 2 teaspoons chopped parsley and then mix everything together well. Now I form it into patties and broil them for about 3 minutes on each side, or until they start to brown. You can also fry them in some light vegetable oil if you want, but that is more fattening and the taste isn't that different.

My mother always served the patties with boiled red potatoes with butter and sour cream on them. What a gas! Try it sometime.

TUNA FISH CASSEROLE

ABOUT 4 SERVINGS

½ pound fresh tuna
3 tablespoons butter
3 tablespoones whole-wheat
  flour

1½ cups milk
Leftover cooked asparagus or
  other vegetable
¾ cup sliced mushrooms

½ cup chopped celery
2 tablespoons butter
1 ½ cups sesame noodles
Spring water
1 small onion
1 pimento, chopped

½ teaspoon salt
¼ teaspoon pepper
1 tablespoon chopped parsley
½ cup fresh peas
⅓ cup sunflower seeds

Broil the tuna until it will flake. (I use tuna fillets and broil them about 3 minutes on each side.) Now clean the flesh out from the skin and flake it into a large bowl.

The object of this dish is to use up leftover vegetables that have accumulated over a couple days. I love to make this dish when I have asparagus. I make a cream sauce by melting the butter, stirring in the flour and adding the milk, stirring till the sauce thickens. When the sauce is thick, I add the leftover vegetable. While the sauce is simmering over a very low flame, I sauté the mushrooms and celery in butter until they get tender, then add them to the cream sauce.

Now I put the sesame noodles on to boil in spring water, and while they are cooking I chop up an onion and add it to the cream sauce. Now I add the pimento, salt, pepper, and parsley to the sauce and it is ready. When the noodles are ready I add them to the sauce with the peas and tuna fish, and toss it all up. When everything is mixed up well, I pour it into a large casserole and put the sunflower seeds on top. Then I bake it at about 350° for 25 to 30 minutes.

Traif

This is the section that I call "Traif." All the recipes in this section contain ingredients that are taboo in a kosher Jewish home. However, my rationalization is that I am a modern Jewish woman who has risen above the old silly customs. Besides, I love shellfish so much that I really don't think that I could ever give it up completely. I try to keep it to once a week, but when the crab meat is cheap you might find me gobbling it down almost every day for a week until I just have to have a rest. A question that may come up in your mind is, How did she ever start eating that stuff if she came from a good kosher home? Well, the truth is that although my grandmother (who lived with us until I was about nine) ran a good kosher home, my mother thought that she was very modern for her times, too, and it was Mother who turned me on to it. Can you believe that, my own Jewish mother did it to me. . . .

CRAB-TOMATO CASSEROLE

ABOUT 4 SERVINGS

2 *crabs, hard-shelled*
1 *medium onion, chopped*
½ *green pepper, chopped*
1 *tablespoon butter*

2 *tablespoons chopped parsley*
½ *teaspoon salt*
¼ *teaspoon pepper*

2 tablespoons whole-wheat
flour
4 tomatoes, peeled and
chopped (Make sure that
they are real ripe)

¼ teaspoon thyme
¼ teaspoon tarragon
½ cup rye cracker crumbs
Sesame seeds

Cook the crabs as you do lobster in the next recipe, and when they are cool remove all the meat. Don't forget the claws—they have the tenderest meat of all. Sauté the onion and the green pepper in the butter. Now add the flour to the sautéed vegetables and mix it until a paste forms. Mix in all the other ingredients except the sesame seeds. Put into a buttered baking dish and sprinkle the top with some sesame seeds. Bake at 375° for 20 minutes. Serve hot, with Herb Rice (page 48) on the side.

LOBSTER-CHEESE CASSEROLE

2–3 SERVINGS

1 live lobster
½ pound mushrooms
6 tablespoons butter
2 tablespoons arrowroot
starch
1½ cups cream
1 teaspoon dry mustard
½ cup grated Parmesan

cheese (I often use Monterey Jack)
½ teaspoon salt
2 tablespoons chopped parsley
¼ cup rye cracker crumbs
¼ cup sunflower seeds

Plunge the lobster, head first, into a large pot of rapidly boiling salted water. Return to a boil, cover, and boil 12 to 15 minutes. When the lobster is cool enough to handle, remove all the meat that you can get to. (If you can't get fresh lobster, do what you have to, just don't tell me about it.) Clean and slice the mushrooms and sauté them in 2 tablespoons of the butter. Make a cream sauce by melting 2 tablespoons of the butter, stirring in the arrowroot starch with a whisk, and adding the cream, stirring constantly until the sauce begins to thicken. Then add the mustard and the cheese and stir with the whisk until the cheese is melted and the sauce is smooth. Stir in the salt and the parsley.

Toast the cracker crumbs in the remaining butter. Add the mushrooms and the lobster to the sauce and pour it into a casserole dish. Sprinkle the top with the cracker crumbs and the sunflower seeds and bake at 400° for 15 minutes.

This same dish can be prepared with shrimp or crabmeat instead of lobster, or with a combination.

Herb Rice (page 48) makes a nice side dish with the lobster.

SHRIMP AND BANANA CURRY

ABOUT 4 SERVINGS

1 *pound fresh shrimp*
Boiling salted spring water
4 *tablespoons butter*
4 *tablespoons arrowroot*
   starch or whole-wheat
   flour

2 *cups milk*
1–1½ *teaspoons curry pow-*
   der (You taste as you put
   it in)
2 *slightly ripe bananas*
4 *cups cooked Correct*
   Brown Rice (page 47)

Cook the shrimp for 3 minutes in boiling salted spring water. When they turn pink, remove them and drain them. When they are cool enough, peel and devein them and set them aside. In a skillet, melt the butter and stir in the flour till a paste forms. Now add the milk, stirring constantly with a wire whisk until the sauce begins to thicken. Add the curry powder, and please be careful not to put too much in. Add a little at a time until it is right. (I don't like heavy curry dishes, and believe me it is very easy to go from just right to disgusting in just a few sprinkles.) Now slice the bananas into the sauce and keep stirring. When the bananas begin to soften a little, add the shrimp and simmer for about 10 minutes, or until the shrimp get hot.

Serve right away, over brown rice that you have hopefully had cooking since before you started this dish. A good time to have started the rice would have been when the shrimp were done boiling.

SHRIMP DE JONGUE

ABOUT 4 SERVINGS

3 pounds fresh shrimp
1 clove garlic (I use 2, but I like lots and lots of gralic)
¾ cup butter, at room temperature
1 teaspoon salt
¼ teaspoon tarragon
¼ teaspoon marjoram

¼ cup chopped parsley
1 cup bread or cracker crumbs (I use Swedish rye crackers from the health food store and grind them up in my blender, because I rarely have any old bread in the house)

Boil the shrimp for 3 to 5 minutes and then peel and devein; or else use shrimp that have already been cooked. (Just remember that you won't need 3 pounds of cooked shrimp. They weigh less after they have been cooked. I would use only 2 pounds if I bought frozen cooked shrimp.)

Mash the garlic. (I use a mortar and pestle to do mine, because I have never found a garlic press that I liked. They never do their job as far as I'm concerned. Anyway, I mash the garlic up with my mortar and pestle until it is pasty.) Put the garlic in a bowl and add the softened butter. Mush them together until the garlic is well distributed throughout the butter. Add the salt, tarragon, marjoram, and 1 teaspoon of the parsley and cream everything together till they are well blended. Add the cracker crumbs and squish everything together until they are all blended together well. (I use my hand for squishing because it works so well.)

Place a layer of shrimp in a buttered casserole dish and top with a layer of the crumb mixture. Sprinkle with some of the parsley. Continue alternating the layers until everything is in the casserole, remembering to sprinkle the parsley over the mixture whenever the crumb mixture is added. (*Don't* forget the parsley. I have a habit of doing that, and it is so frustrating.) Bake at 400° for 20 to 25 minutes.

SHRIMP IN TOMATOES

4–5 SERVINGS

2 *pounds fresh shrimp*
1 *large onion, chopped*
1 *green pepper, chopped*
1 *cup chopped celery*
3 *tablespoons butter*
7 *very ripe tomatoes, peeled*
3 *tablespoons arrowroot starch*

½ *teaspoon salt*
¼ *teaspoon white pepper*
1 *teaspoon basil*
1 *teaspoon chopped parsley*
½ *cup black olives*
4 *cups Correct Brown Rice (page 47)*

This is one of the old standards that I just can't give up. Drop the shrimp into boiling water and boil for 3 to 5 minutes, and then, when they are cool, peel and devein them. Sauté the onion, green pepper, and celery in the butter until they are tender. Add the tomatoes and sort of break them up a bit, then add a little of the arrowroot starch as a thickener and stir it in well. Add more only if you need it. (You may not need it all, depending on how juicy the tomatoes are.) Add the salt, pepper, basil, and parsley and then the shrimp. Stir it a little and then put a very low flame under the pan. Simmer it for 5 to 10 minutes, but not much longer because the shrimp will get tough if you leave them in too long. Right before you are going to serve it, add the olives and let them warm up a bit. Serve it over brown rice, which I hope you thought of starting right after the shrimp were through boiling.

HOT SHELLFISH CASSEROLE

4–5 SERVINGS

1 *pound fresh shrimp*
2 *quarts boiling salted water*
1 *fresh crab*
2 *cups Correct Brown Rice (page 47)*
2 *tablespoons butter*
2 *medium onions, chopped*
1 *green pepper, chopped*
2 *cups sliced fresh mushrooms*

¼ *teaspoon thyme*
½ *teaspoon marjoram*
3 *ripe tomatoes, peeled*
1½ *teaspoons chili powder*
1 *cup cream*
Sprinkle of paprika
Sesame seeds (optional)

Cook the shrimp by dropping them into 2 quarts boiling salted water and allowing them to boil for 3 to 5 minutes. As soon as they turn pink, you will know that they are ready to come out. Remove them from the water and cool them with cold tap water. Then peel and devein them. Cook the crab by lobster method (page 107). (Seeing as I live in San Francisco, I always can buy the crab freshly cooked at the wharf or in Chinatown. I never have had to throw a live crab into boiling water myself, and frankly I choose not to. Thus I just take home the cooked crab and clean out as much of the meat as I can get.) Set the shrimp and crab meat aside.

Put the rice on to cook so it will be ready when you need it. Next melt the butter in a skillet and slowly sauté the onion, green pepper, and mushrooms in it. Place the vegetables into a deep casserole dish and cover them with the rice. Now add the seafood and sprinkle it with the thyme and marjoram. Chop up the tomatoes and place them on top of the seafood. Mix the chili powder with the cream and pour it over the casserole. Sprinkle the top with paprika and some sesame seeds, if you want, and bake at 375° for 20 minutes.

This is a nice spicy dish, but all the ingredients together make it a real winner. If you don't want to use the chili powder, you can substitute cayenne pepper or leave it out completely.

Salads

There is one note that I feel the need to make here. In every one of my salads I use some nuts or seeds. If I haven't mentioned it in the recipe, it is only because I don't want to force you into thinking that you have to use them, too. I just want you to know that I think that, since I depend on them so much for one of my protein sources, it is important to eat as many seeds and nuts as possible. So remember, if you don't find some kind of seeds or nuts in a certain salad recipe, that doesn't mean that I'm not using them. You can do whatever you like as far as they go, just try them on a few different salads to see if you like them before making any judgment.

Sprouts are another ingredient that belongs in most vegetables and fruit salads. If I don't mention it as an ingredient in a salad, it is probably because I forgot, or else I was afraid you might not like it with that particular salad. Just keep in mind that a handful of fresh sprouts should go on top, or alongside, all the salads that you make.

THE BIG SALAD

When I make a salad it usually is a variation in some way of the following ingredients. Some are left out at different times of the year, depending on their availability. A salad of just lettuce and cucumbers is very nice sometimes, and that may be enough for some people. I often eat just some cucumber slices with a scoop of sour cream on them and that is a salad for that day. Sliced tomatoes with avocado pieces are also good, with a little lemon juice squeezed on them.

Here is the combination that I usually use when I am having a big dinner and I want everyone to really get into the salad.

Lettuce. I rarely use head lettuce (iceberg) any more, because when I was a little girl that was the only kind my mother ever used in her salad. I'm not sure exactly why, but the fact remains that it was the only kind that I was ever exposed to until I left home at the age of twenty and began to learn about things for myself. Thus now I use a variety of butter lettuce, red tip lettuce (my favorite), sometimes romaine, and whatever else happens to be in season. I am sure that you already know this, but I will mention it anyway. Never cut lettuce with a knife. Always tear it when you are putting it into a salad.

Tomatoes. My favorite; when tomatoes are out of season, or, even worse, when they are no good, I am very sad. To me, a salad without a tomato isn't really a salad.

Cucumber. For some reason the cucumbers in this part of the country have been really crummy lately. However, when they are nice and not too expensive you should take advantage of them. You can always cut in some fresh zucchini instead, if you can't find some nice cucumbers.

Green onions. I usually chop up a few, but not too many. Sometimes my mood changes, and I use red onions for a while.

Radishes. Just a few for color and flavor.

Mushrooms. A few fresh mushrooms in the salad are a treat.

Green pepper. I cut it up into small pieces for color and flavor.

Avocado. Great sliced on top of the salad.

Artichoke hearts. Also served on top, and are they ever yummy. This is one of the items that I buy in the supermarket. They come in a little jar, marinated in olive oil and herbs.

Olives. Once in a while for a little variety.

This, then, is the average salad that I serve, give or take a vege-table or two. The choice is always up to you—try and remember that.

SALAD VARIATION # 1

4–6 SERVINGS

1½ heads of lettuce, leaves torn into desired-size pieces
½ pound zucchini, cut up
1 turnip, diced
1 cauliflower, broken into pieces
3 stalks of celery, chopped

4 green onions, chopped, ends and all
4 carrots, sliced
3 tomatoes, cut into sections
1 green pepper, chopped
Some fresh parsley

Arrange the vegetables in a way that suits your eye, and serve them with a dressing that fits the mood.

SALAD VARIATION # 2

4–6 SERVINGS

1 cup dried lima beans
2 cups shelled peas
Salted spring water
2 cups sliced green beans
2 cups chopped celery

2 cups chopped carrots
2 cups sliced zucchini
Sunflower seeds
Oil and vinegar

Soak the lima beans overnight. In the morning place them in salted spring water and cook them until they are tender. It takes about 30 minutes.

Now steam all the other vegetables in a vegetable steamer or cook them whatever way you usually do it, only don't let them get too soft. The crisper they are, the better. When they are done, mix them with the lima beans and put them into the refrigerator to chill for a hour or so. When you are ready to serve the salad, toss it with a little oil and vinegar dressing, very little because you don't want the vegetables to get soggy. Right before serving, sprinkle the salad with some sunflower seeds.

FARMER'S CHOP SUEY

ABOUT 4 GOOD SERVINGS

1 cucumber, sliced and quar-
tered
4 cups chopped lettuce
1 cup chopped red cabbage
1 cup sliced carrots
1 bunch green onions,
chopped

1 pint sour cream
1 tablespoon salt
1 teaspoon pepper
¼ cup sunflower seeds (optional)
1 handful sprouts (optional)

Put all the vegetables in a big bowl. Mix the sour cream, salt, and pepper. Pour over the vegetables and toss well. Add the sunflower seeds and sprouts. Serve right away, before the vegetables can get mushy from the cream mixture.

SESAME-ASPARAGUS SALAD

4–6 SERVINGS

2 pounds asparagus
¼ cup soy sauce
2 tablespoons sesame oil
¼ cup sesame seeds

¼ teaspoon honey
Lettuce leaves
Bean sprouts

Cut the asparagus into small pieces and steam them until they are tender (about 5 minutes). Remove from the steamer and drain them well. Chill for about 1 hour. Mix ¼ cup soy sauce with the oil, the seeds, and the honey and marinate the asparagus in the mixture for at least another hour. Serve on a bed of lettuce leaves, topped by fresh bean sprouts and sprinkled with extra soy sauce before serving.

ARNELLE'S COLE SLAW

4–6 SERVINGS

1 head cabbage
3 carrots
3 green onions
1 ½ cups mayonnaise
½ cup sour cream
3 tablespoons vinegar (Use your favorite: it's good

with cider vinegar, which is what I use, but I've had it with red wine vinegar, too, and it is also good)
Salt and pepper to taste
Paprika (optional)

This recipe comes from my friend Arnelle, who is one of the best cooks in San Francisco.

Grate the cabbage and the carrots and chop the onions. Place all the vegetables in a bowl. Mix the mayonnaise, sour cream, and vinegar, and add salt and pepper to suit your taste. Mix all the above ingredients well, and pour over the vegetables. Toss everything up good and sprinkle a little paprika over the top, if you like it. (I don't use the paprika all the time. Just when I want to make it look special.)

PAMM'S COLE SLAW

4–6 SERVINGS

1 head cabbage
3–4 carrots
½ small onion

1 cup mayonnaise
½ teaspoon salt
¼ teaspoon pepper

2 *teaspoons vinegar*   Paprika (*optional*)
¼ *cup honey*

Grate the cabbage, carrots, and onion into a bowl. In a separate bowl mix the mayonnaise, salt, pepper, and vinegar. Now slowly add the honey, mixing well. Don't add all of it at once! A little at a time, and be sure and taste it as you add and mix. (You may not need all of the honey I've suggested. My sister, who just happens to be Pamm, uses sugar [½ cup], but, seeing as I don't use any sugar in my cooking, I had to convert to honey. Honey is much heavier and more condensed than sugar, so you never need as much honey as sugar. Thus I reduced the amount by half, but, depending on the type of honey you use, you may not need it all. This recipe is great, though. It is Pamm's specialty. As a matter of fact, she only has two specialties. The other is meat loaf, and you know, I'm sure, where I stand on that one. . . .)

Anyway, mix the sauce over the vegetables and toss well. Sprinkle with a little paprika, if you like, and put it into the refrigerator to chill for at least 2 hours before serving.

SOY-CABBAGE SALAD

6–8 SERVINGS

5 *hard-boiled eggs*   1 *large or* 2 *small heads cab-*
½ *cup mayonnaise*   *bage, cut up in chunks*
1 *teaspoon salt*   2–3 *cups cooked soybeans*
½ *teaspoon pepper*   1 *bunch green onions,*
½ *teaspoon paprika*   *chopped*
                             Sunflower seeds (*optional*)

Mush up the eggs in the mayonnaise; add the salt, pepper, and ½ teaspoon paprika and mix. Combine the cabbage chunks with the soybeans and the chopped onions. Pour the dressing over the mixture and toss well. Sprinkle with a few sunflower seeds, if you'd like, and shake a little bit more of the paprika on top for color.

CARROT SALAD

4–6 SERVINGS

5 carrots, chopped
1 cup chopped nuts (either almonds or walnuts, or a combination of both)
½ cup sunflower seeds

1 cup alfalfa sprouts
½ cup raisins (optional)
1–1½ cups mayonnaise or yogurt

Mix all the ingredients and pour the yogurt or mayonnaise over it and toss.

This makes a great salad for an evening when you can't face a lettuce-base salad. I use the yogurt when I make it, and I think that it has a lighter taste. Try it both ways and decide for yourself. You can add chopped celery to the salad, or substitute it for the carrots.

CAULIFLOWER-AVOCADO SALAD

4–6 SERVINGS

1 head cauliflower
2 very ripe avocados, peeled and pitted
¼ cup cider vinegar
6 tablespoons light vegetable oil

1 teaspoon salt
Dash of pepper
½ cup chopped almonds
1 tomato, peeled
Lettuce leaves
Radishes for garnish

Steam the cauliflower in your steamer, or cook it in whatever way you please. While it is steaming, combine the peeled and pitted avocados with the vinegar, oil, salt, and pepper in your blender. Blend them all together and then add the almonds for another quick whiz. Chop up the tomato and add it to the avocado mixture, and whiz again. Remove from the blender.

When the cauliflower is done, remove it and chill it for about an hour. When you are ready to serve it, pour the dressing over it, after you have placed it on a bed of lettuce leaves. Garnish with radishes.

CUCUMBERS IN SOUR CREAM
AT LEAST 6 SERVINGS

3 cucumbers
1 medium Bermuda onion
1 ½ tablespoons salt
1 ½ cups sour cream

3 tablespoons vinegar
½ teaspoon fresh pepper
1 tablespoon chopped chives

Peel and slice the cucumbers and the onion thin and pour the salt over them in a bowl. Let them sit for a few hours in the refrigerator. Next rinse them and strain out the liquid. Mix the sour cream, vinegar, pepper, and chives and put the mixture over the cucumbers. Stir it in and then chill again for a while.

The same recipe can be prepared with yogurt, only leave out the vinegar.

TOMATO AND COTTAGE CHEESE

This salad was a very popular number around my house as I was growing up. My mother and I ate this salad quite often during the summer months when it was just too hot to think of anything else to make. Unfortunately, my sister wasn't into tomatoes or cottage cheese, so she would have a can of spaghetti—straight from the can—when we ate this salad. Can you imagine that, cold spaghetti? Those noodles always reminded me of slimy worms, and the color of the sauce! well, there just isn't any way to describe that.

For each salad:

1 *large tomato*
1 *large lettuce leaf*
1 *teaspoon chopped chives*
1 *cup cottage cheese*

2 *teaspoons sesame seeds or*
   chopped nuts
Salt

Cut the tomato in sections and open it like a flower onto the lettuce leaf. Mix the chives into the cottage cheese and scoop it into the tomato. Sprinkle the seeds or nuts on top and season with a little salt.

This is how I like to eat it, but, if you want, you can serve it with a dressing of some kind. I suggest a light avocado dressing (such as the one on page 128). Serve some fresh sprouts with it if you have some.

PICNIC POTATO SALAD

6–8 SERVINGS

10 *medium potatoes*
Lightly salted spring water
1 *cup mayonnaise*
¼ *cup sour cream (I some-*
   times use a little more)
1½ *teaspoons dry mustard*
1½ *teaspoons salt*

½ *teaspoon pepper*
Chopped parsley
¼ *cup cider vinegar*
1 *cup chopped celery*
1 *cup chopped green onions,*
   with the tops
Paprika

Boil the potatoes in lightly salted spring water until they are soft. Remove the jackets and let them cool. While the potatoes are cooling, make the dressing.

Combine the mayonnaise with the sour cream, mustard, salt, pepper, 2 tablespoons parsley, and any other spices you may want to add. Now add the vinegar and stir well. Pour the mixture over the celery and the onions and mix it up, then cut up the potatoes and place in a large bowl. Pour the sauce mixture over the potatoes and toss it all up. Sprinkle it with a bit of paprika and a little extra parsley. You can refrigerate it now for a while, if you like cold salads. I don't, so I just leave it out at room temperature.

ZUCCHINI SALAD

4–6 SERVINGS

6 zucchini, sliced thin
2 tomatoes, chopped into small pieces
1 green pepper, chopped
1 small onion, chopped
½ cup sunflower seeds
½ teaspoon honey
1 teaspoon salt
½ teaspoon pepper
¼ teaspoon paprika
½ cup fresh sprouts
Lettuce leaves
Oil and vinegar or lemon juice

As you cut up the vegetables, place them into a bowl. Toss them around a bit and add the seeds, tossing them in, too. Now add the honey, salt, pepper, and paprika, toss again, and put the sprouts on top of the salad. Scoop out servings onto a bed of lettuce leaves and serve with a mild vinegar- and oil-base dressing or with plain lemon juice.

AVOCADO STUFFED

1 SERVING

1 avocado
1 lettuce leaf
1 cup cottage cheese
1 teaspoon chopped chives
2 teaspoons chopped almonds or walnuts

Cut the avocado in half, spoon it out from its skin, and place it on the lettuce leaf. Mix the cottage cheese with the chives and spoon it onto the avocado. Sprinkle the nuts on top, and top them with a scoop of mayonnaise, or any other dressing that you may have in mind.

This can be a filling meal if you have a few crackers to eat along with it. I like this especially for lunch, because it isn't *too* fattening, and I find it very satisfying. To make it a little more interesting, you could add a few slices of your favorite cheese to the plate.

AVOCADOS AND ORANGES

3–4 SERVINGS

Lettuce leaves
2 avocados, peeled and pitted
2 cups orange sections
½ cup chopped walnuts

Lay a bed of lettuce leaves on a plate, slice the avocados into strips, and lay them on the lettuce. Cover with the orange sections and the walnuts and your favorite light oil-base dressing. (I don't use any dressing on this at all, I just sort of mush the avocados onto the orange slices and that's good enough for me.)

PEAR AND AVOCADO SALAD

4–6 SERVINGS

4 pears, peeled or not, cut up in chunks
2 stalks of celery, chopped
1 ripe avocado, peeled and cut up into chunks
1 cup chopped walnuts or pecans
½ cup sunflower seeds
½ cup raisins (optional)
1 cup yogurt or mayonnaise

Place all the ingredients in a bowl, and add the yogurt or the mayonnaise. (I strongly advise the use of the yogurt, because it is much easier to digest and a lot less fattening.)

YOGURT À LA WALDORF

AT LEAST 4 SERVINGS

Do you remember those old Girl Scout days, when every time there was some kind of an occasion where they served a salad it was that awful Waldorf thing just smothered with straight mayonnaise and oh, it was bad? It also was a popular number on the sweet sixteen circuit. I used to get sick whenever I saw it coming. Well, if you take the same basic ingredients and just substitute yogurt for the mayonnaise, I think you will have a pleasant surprise. The yogurt is much better for you than the mayonnaise, and the salad takes on a whole new perspective with this small change.

4 *cups diced apples (Use different kinds of apples for variety if they are available)*
2 *cups chopped celery*
1½ *cups chopped walnuts*
(or pecans, if you are rich)
1½ *tablespoons honey (optional; I don't use it myself)*
1¼ *cups plain yogurt*
Sprouts

Toss the apples with the celery and the nuts until they are all mixed up pretty well. Mix the honey into the yogurt if you are going to use it and then pour it over the salad. Toss everything together well, add some sprouts on the top before serving, and then serve it. You can refrigerate it for an hour or so if you want to. (I don't care for cold fruit or vegetables because they do funny things to my teeth. I guess I am sensitive that way, because nothing else bothers me the way cold fruit and vegetables do. Anyway, I don't refrigerate it before I serve it.) By the way, if you do refrigerate it, be sure to cover the bowl so that the apples don't start to turn brown around the edges.

JUMBO FRUIT SALAD

4–6 SERVINGS

2 *cups grapefruit sections*
2 *cups orange sections*
3 *peaches, sliced*
1 *cup Concord grapes (Don't worry about the seeds, eat them—they can't hurt you)*
1 *pineapple, cut up*

1 *honeydew melon, cut up or in balls*
3 *pears, cut up in chunks*
Yogurt or dressing (see below)
Shredded coconut
Chopped walnuts

Don't stop with the fruits I've given you. If plums are in season, throw a few of them in. Same goes for strawberries and blueberries. I serve yogurt on top of the fruit mixture, but there is a different dressing that you can use if you want to (see below). Pour whatever you use over the salad and toss it up. Now sprinkle some shredded coconut and a few chopped walnuts on top and serve.

1 *cup cream*
Honey
Vanilla extract

½ *cup mayonnaise*
2 *tablespoons orange juice*

First whip up the cream with a little honey and a drop of vanilla extract. When it is thick enough, add the mayonnaise and the orange juice and whip it some more.

CITRUS SALAD

3–4 SERVINGS

Lettuce leaves
2 *cups grapefruit sections*
2 *cups orange sections*

¼ *cup shredded coconut*
1 *cup chopped celery*
½ *cup sunflower seeds*

On lettuce leaves, arrange some grapefruit and orange sections and sprinkle with shredded coconut. Add some chopped celery and sunflower seeds and serve. (I like to put a scoop of yogurt on top of it, and you can use a light lemon-juice-base dressing, too, if you like.)

Salad Dressings, Pickles, and Relishes

Salad Dressings

All my salad dressings are made in my blender. There is no substitute for the results. I have been developing my love for cooking for at least five years now, and the one thing that I never had much luck with was salad dressings. They were always too vinegary or too something, and I had a real complex about making them. My best trick was to have *almost* everything ready for dinner when my friends would arrive so that whoever was first to come would undoubtedly offer to help with something. You know the old line, "Is there anything I can do to help?" Well, instead of graciously replying, "Oh, no, just go in and relax," I would say, "Sure, how about making the salad dressing?" It always got me out of trouble, until finally I started to feel bad because I couldn't make a decent salad dressing of my own even if I followed a recipe.

Anyway, here are a few recipes that I have managed to put together from other suggestions, and I hope you find them a bit useful.

CREAMY MAYONNAISE

ABOUT 1 CUP

½ cup mayonnaise
¼ cup sour cream
¼ cup light oil
2 tablespoons cider vinegar
1 teaspoon chopped parsley
Pinch of salt
Smaller pinch of pepper
½ teaspoon salad herbs (This is a combination of basil, thyme, tarragon, marjoram, and a few others that come already bottled for your convenience. I like to use them because it definitely saves time and energy)
Pinch of garlic salt (optional)

Combine all the ingredients in the blender and just whiz it around a bit. If you do use garlic salt, be careful not to put in too much, because the mayonnaise really takes up the flavor and a bit too much can ruin the dressing. Use a rubber spatula to push the ingredients down every few seconds to make sure that everything mixes well. (Don't stick it into the blender when it is going, though, because you will have rubber-chunk dressing then, and that kind isn't too popular with most people. I know!) When it is blended well, pour it into a bottle, one with a top, in which you can store it. If it appears to be too thick, add a little spring water and whiz the blender again for a few seconds more, until it is a bit thinner. Good on most salads.

CREAM GARLIC DRESSING

This is the one that they call "Green Goddess" in the fancy restaurants. The food coloring has been left out for obvious reasons; I'm sure I don't have to go into them.

ABOUT 1 CUP

½ cup mayonnaise
½ cup sour cream (or try it
    with yogurt)
½ teaspoon garlic powder
Pinch of salt

Pinch of pepper
1 teaspoon honey
½ teaspoon celery salt
1 tablespoon vinegar or
    lemon juice

Combine all the ingredients in the blender, and thin with spring water if necessary.

AVOCADO DRESSING

ABOUT ¾ CUP

1 very ripe avocado
2 tablespoons mayonnaise
2 tablespoons lemon juice
½ teaspoon salt

1 tablespoon minced onion
3 tablespoons ground sun-
    flower seeds or 5 walnuts,
    ground

Put all the ingredients in the blender and whiz them around until they are well blended. (Thin with a little spring water if you want to, but I don't suggest that you do. This dressing is fine the thicker it is.)

SESAME-SEED DRESSING

ABOUT 1 CUP

½ cup light vegetable oil
¼ cup vinegar (I use cider
    vinegar)

1 teaspoon salt
¼ cup honey
¼ cup sesame seeds

Put everything except half the sesame seeds into the blender and whiz it up. When all the ingredients are mixed well, pour the dressing into a bowl and add the remaining seeds. Stir them in and there is your dressing.

DOCTORED-UP FRENCH DRESSING
ABOUT 1⅓ CUPS

1 cup olive oil
⅓ cup cider vinegar
½ teaspoon salt

¼ teaspoon freshly ground pepper

This is the basic recipe for French dressing, and if you like it this way, fine—then go ahead and use it. All you do is mix the salt, pepper, and vinegar and put them into your blender. Now, while the blender is on low speed, slowly add the oil until it is mixed well with the vinegar and spices.

This is very good, but I like a few extras in my French dressing, so this is what I do after I have gotten it to this point. I add:

½ teaspoon mustard powder
Pinch of garlic

Handful of sunflower seeds
½ teaspoon salad herbs

Now, when all these things are in the blender, I whiz it until they are all mixed in and then I thin it down with a little spring water, if it needs to be thinned, and pour it into a bottle for serving.

COTTAGE-CHEESE DRESSING
ABOUT 2¼ CUPS

1½ cups cottage cheese
½ cup milk
1 tablespoon chopped chives
2 tablespoons chopped pars-

ley
½ teaspoon salt
¼ teaspoon freshly ground pepper

¼ cup walnuts or sunflower
    seeds

2 green onions, chopped
    (without the greens)

Place the cottage cheese and the milk in your blender and whiz until they are creamy. Add the remaining ingredients and blend them into the cottage cheese mixture until they are well distributed. Place in a covered container and use as a low-calorie dressing on your different salads.

YOGURT DRESSING

ABOUT 1 CUP

There is no doubt that yogurt is perfect just the way it is on top of any fruit or vegetable salad. However, this is a special dressing that you can make easily when you want to impress someone.

1 cup yogurt
1 teaspoon lemon juice
1 teaspoon chopped chives
1 teaspoon chopped parsley

½ teaspoon salt
¼ teaspoon pepper
½ teaspoon dry mustard
Handful of sunflower seeds

Combine all the ingredients in your blender, and whiz them around until they are well blended. This dressing should be refrigerated before using. (If you want a sweeter dressing, you can substitute 1 teaspoon of honey for the lemon juice.)

NUT DRESSING

ABOUT 1⅓ CUPS

Big handful of nuts (Either almonds, walnuts, or pecans will do fine. A big handful usually amounts to

from 15 to 20 nuts. The more the better, as far as I'm concerned)
2 cloves garlic

½ *teaspoon salt*   1 *cup olive oil*
¼ *teaspoon white pepper*   ⅓ *cup vinegar*

If you are using almonds, blanch them by pouring boiling water over them in a bowl and then rubbing the skins off immediately. Dry the nuts right away, so that the water doesn't saturate them. Now put the nuts in the blender with the garlic cloves and run it until they combine. Add the salt and the pepper and pour the oil in slowly while the blender is running at low speed. When all the oil is in, add the vinegar and give it a quick whiz until it combines with the rest of the mixture.

THOUSAND ISLAND DRESSING
ABOUT 2 ¼ CUPS

While I was growing up my only encounter with Thousand Island dressing was a strong mixture of mayonnaise and catsup with lots of Worcestershire sauce in it. Needless to say, I didn't like it too much, and that was unfortunate because it happened to be the only home-made salad dressing that my mother made. I hope she will forgive me for telling you all this, but it was because of this that I didn't develop a real taste for salads until I left home. Bottled dressings were the other choice, and most of the time the only one we had was a reddish-color one optimistically called "French dressing." It is so sweet, but it was my sister's favorite and she was such a fussy eater. Thus it was the one that my mother bought in order to get Pamm to at least eat something.

Anyway, here is a recipe for Thousand Island that I think is a little better that the usual kind that I got as a kid.

1 ½ *cups mayonnaise*   1 *small tomato, peeled and*
¼ *cup chopped parsley*   *chopped*
¼ *cup chopped olives*   ½ *clove garlic*
¼ *cup chopped chives*   ¼ *green pepper, chopped*
3 *tablespoons chopped pi-*   1 *tablespoon cider vinegar*
   mento

Place all the ingredients in your blender and whiz them up until they are blended. If the dressing is a bit too thin, add 1 or 2 teaspoons of arrowroot starch and stir it into the mixture. Don't blend it in with the blender, *stir* it in.

RUSSIAN DRESSING

ABOUT 2½ CUPS

1 *cup ripe tomatoes, peeled*
¾ *cup oil (I prefer light vegetable oil)*
½ *clove garlic*
½ *small onion, cut up in pieces*
3 *tablespoons honey*

1 *tablespoon salt*
1 *tablespoon dry mustard*
½ *teaspoon paprika*
¼ *cup lemon juice*
¼ *cup cider vinegar*
¼ *cup sesame or poppy seeds*

Put all the ingredients except the seeds in the blender and whiz it until the dressing is well combined. Use a spatula to push down the excess from the sides. Now if the dressing is too thin, add 1 teaspoon of arrowroot starch and run the blender for a few seconds. If it is thick enough, fine, otherwise add another teaspoon and run again. Now add the seeds and whiz a few seconds, then pour the dressing into a bottle for storing.

QUICK HERB DRESSING

Prepare one of the mayonnaise recipes (see page 26) in a quantity to suit your needs, and then add some of your favorite herbs, for instance:

Basil   *Chives*
Parsley   *Garlic*

A pinch of each of the above to suit your taste, and you have a nice simple dressing for a salad.

You can add orégano or marjoram or rosemary as a substitute or in addition to the basil, depending on your taste. And before adding the dressing to the salad, you might want to squeeze a little extra lemon juice over the vegetables.

PICKLED CUCUMBERS

4–6 SERVINGS

2 *medium cucumbers, peeled and sliced thin*
1 *onion, sliced thin*
1 *green pepper, sliced in thin rings*

1 ½ *teaspoons salt*
¼ *teaspoon pepper*
¾ *cup vinegar*
½ *teaspoon honey*
½ *cup spring water*

Arrange the vegetables in layers in a bowl. Sprinkle salt and pepper over each layer. Mix the vinegar, honey, and spring water and pour it over the vegetables. Chill the vegetables for about 3 hours. Serve as is, in the liquid.

PICKLED VEGETABLES

4–5 QUARTS

1 *cup chopped red pepper*
1 *cup chopped green pepper*
1 *cup chopped onion*
3 *cups peeled, diced beets*
2 *cups chopped green beans*
2 *cups chopped cauliflower*
2 *cups cider vinegar*

1 *tablespoon salt*
¼ *cup honey*
1 *tablespoon dry mustard*
2 *teaspoons pickling spices*
1 *clove garlic*
Spring water

Put all the cut-up vegetables in a saucepan. Mix the vinegar, salt, honey, mustard, and pickling spices, and pour it over the vegetables. Add the garlic clove, and bring the mixture to a boil. Reduce the heat and cook over a low heat for 10 minutes, stirring occasionally. Put the mixture evenly into jars, and fill the jars to the rim with spring water. Seal tightly and chill right away. Leave them in the refrigerator for about 2 days.

DILL PICKLES

ABOUT 4 QUARTS

3 *dozen small pickling cu-cumbers*
Garlic cloves
Bay leaves

4 *tablespoons salt*
2 *teaspoons dill*
1 *tablespoon pickling spices*
Spring water

Clean the cucumbers, then pack them in glass jars that have been sterilized. Place 3 cloves of garlic and 1 large bay leaf in each jar.

Mix the salt, dill, and pickling spices up together and divide them evenly among the jars.

Fill each jar to the brim with spring water. Seal the jars tightly and store them in a cool, dark place for at least 2 weeks. This is one of those things that are better when you let them sit as long as you can.

SAUERKRAUT

ABOUT 3 PINTS

8 *cups shredded green cab-bage*
4 *tablespoons sea salt*

1 *tablespoon caraway seeds*
Spring water

Place the cabbage in a large bowl. Sprinkle the salt over the cabbage and toss it well. Mix in the seeds, and let the mixture stand for 1 hour.

Pack the cabbage mixture into sterile glass jars and fill to the brim with spring water. Store the jars in a cool, dark place for about a month. (A good idea for this and other put-up foods, is to paint pretty pictures on the lids with model-kit enamel paint, which you can get cheaply in any dime store, and then give the jars of food as gifts. Wait and see, you'll be a real hit with your friends.)

PIMENTOS

Pimentos are very good in salads and in different casseroles, especially tuna fish casserole. They are easy to make on your own, so why not give it a try?

Get some nice sweet red peppers when they are in season and real cheap. Wash them and drain them well, and then place them on a cookie sheet. Now place the cookie sheet under your broiler and broil them at about 400°, watching them carefully and turning them constantly until their skins begin to blister all over. Be careful not to burn them. All you want to do is get those skins soft enough to peel easily. When they have blistered all over, remove them from the broiler and let them cool for a few minutes. When they are cool enough to handle, remove the skins with a knife, then remove the seeds and stems. Now make up a mixture of oil, lemon juice, and salt (see below for amounts) and toss the peppers in it. Let them marinate in the mixture for several hours.

The peppers will now be ready to use, or else you can place them in a jar and store them in the refrigerator. I never make too many peppers at a time, usually never more than three or four. When I make four, I use about ½ cup of oil and ⅓ cup of lemon juice with 1 teaspoon of salt.

Another good use for pimentos is to cut them up in tiny pieces and put them into different dips that you may make when you have guests. I love the flavor that they have, and I have been known to eat a bowl of them straight.

CRANBERRY-ORANGE RELISH

ABOUT 4–6 SERVINGS

1 *pound cranberries*
2 *oranges, sliced, with seeds removed*

¼ *cup honey*
½ *cup hot spring water*

Put the cranberries in the blender and whiz them around. Add the oranges and blend the two together. Place in a saucepan and add the honey and water. Cook over medium heat for 45 minutes.

Place the relish, when cool, in the refrigerator and let it set for at least 3 hours (5 would be better).

Sandwiches, Spreads, and Dips

Sandwiches

Sandwiches are fun and for the most part quite easy to make. I want to just give you a list of the ingredients I use in my sandwiches, and you can take it from there. I never really know exactly what kind of sandwiches I'm going to make until right before I begin to make them. Then I check the refrigerator out and begin. I usually serve a nice home-made soup with a sandwich, or a salad if it's too hot for soup. However, the sandwich is definitely the main course, and everything takes a second place to it.

Bread. You can buy some very good breads in the different health food stores, but I always bake my own.

Mayonnaise. I use Lecithinase, which I buy at the health food store. It tastes just like mayonnaise, but the ingredients are much better for you and it doesn't have any eggs in it. As I have said, I try to eat as little egg as possible, because of the high cholesterol content. It is good to make your own mayonnaise, and I know that it is very easy to do in an electric blender, but for some reason this seems to be one of my lazy points, and, although I try and make my own as often as possible, there is always something else that I would rather do, so I keep a jar of the Lecithinase on hand for my frequent lazy periods.

Mushrooms. Fresh.

Tomatoes.

Avocados.

Sprouts. There are a variety of seeds that can be sprouted, so use whichever one you want. They are all good for you.

Lettuce. Any kind you like; I personally don't like romaine because of its bitter taste.

Olives.

Cottage cheese.

Cheese slices.

Nuts. I find that almonds that have been sliced are the best on sandwiches, but walnuts are good, too. Peanuts and cashews can be ground fresh in the blender to make fantastic nut butters (pages 28–29) that can make wonderful sandwiches, alone or with a bit of jam.

Vegetables. Fresh or any leftover cooked vegetable, say, from the night before, can be added sparingly to any sandwich for extra flavor and appeal.

Fish. Fresh shrimp, crab, tuna, or salmon.

FRIED-EGG SPECIAL

I SANDWICH

If you are still into eggs, then there is no reason why you shouldn't try this combination. Fry an egg in some oil or butter, whichever way you like to do it. Now take about 10 almonds and split them in two. Place some mayonnaise or some Herb Butter (page 141) on the bread that you are going to use (I suggest rye), and place the almonds on top of the spread. Place your egg on top of the almonds and add a slice of tomato or cucumber. Top this with a lettuce leaf and some avocado, if you have it around, and maybe a little salt. How's that?

AVOCADO SPROUT SUPREME

I SANDWICH

When I lived in Chicago, I never even saw an avocado, let alone tasted one, so it took me a long time to develop a taste for them here in California. Now I just love them, and this sandwich is a real turn-on with everyone I give it to.

Mayonnaise
¼ teaspoon dry mustard
2 slices home-made bread
½ large avocado
2 lettuce leaves

2 mushrooms, sliced thin
2 slices tomato
1 small handful sprouts
Salt (optional)

Mix 2 teaspoons of mayonnaise with the mustard and spread some of the mixture on a slice of bread. Arrange the avocado in slices on the bread and add the lettuce and mushrooms and tomato. Add a little more mayonnaise and top with the sprouts. A little salt, if you want, and go to it.

FRESH FISH HEAVEN

I SANDWICH

Mayonnaise to suit
½ teaspoon horseradish
Pinch of chopped parsley
2 lettuce leaves (red tip is good here)
2 ounces fresh seafood (shrimp or crab are best, and at least they are

cheaper than lobster and more elegant than tuna)
2 fresh mushrooms, sliced thin
2 slices bread
Salt (optional)

Mix the mayonnaise, horseradish, and parsley. Arrange the lettuce, seafood, and mushrooms on the bread and spread the mayonnaise mixture on it the way you like. I put it on both pieces of the bread and a little on the seafood, too. Sprinkle on a little salt, if you want it.

START WITH COTTAGE CHEESE

1 SANDWICH

2 slices fresh bread
Mayonnaise or Herb Butter (page 141)
1 lettuce leaf
½ cup cottage cheese
1 teaspoon wheat-germ oil
Handful of walnuts or almonds or both, chopped
Some sunflower seeds (just a small handful)

Salt to taste
½ teaspoon any other herb (like basil, thyme, tarragon, etc., whatever you like)
1 teaspoon chives
1 tomato slice
1 mushroom, sliced

Start with 2 slices of fresh bread. Put some mayonnaise or herb butter on the first slice, or just leave it plain. (I leave the bread plain because I think that there is enough flavor from the cottage cheese with the herbs to satisfy.) Place the lettuce leaf on the bread. Mix the cottage cheese with the wheat-germ oil, and add the chopped nuts and the sunflower seeds. Mix them in with the cheese and then add the salt, herbs, and chives. Mix again, and scoop it onto the lettuce. Pat it down a bit, and then add the tomato slice and the sliced mushrooms. Cover with the second slice of bread and eat.

CHEESE AND NUTS

1 SANDWICH

2 teaspoons mayonnaise (more if you want it)

¼–½ teaspoon dry mustard (optional)

2 *slices bread*
2 *lettuce leaves*
4 *slices cheese (I usually use*
    Monterey Jack or light

Cheddar)
2 *tomato slices*
1 *mushroom, sliced*
10 *almonds, sliced*

Mix the mayonnaise with the mustard, if you want it. Spread some of the mayonnaise or the mayonnaise mixture on a slice of bread. Place a leaf of the lettuce on the bread and top it with the cheese. Place the tomatoes and the mushroom slices on top of the cheese and spread the rest of the mayonnaise on top. Now put the almonds on top of the mayonnaise firmly, to hold them in place. And top with second lettuce leaf and second slice of bread. (I think of it as a gluing process. The object is to try and make the almonds stay on the sandwich when you pick it up. If they don't, well, no problem. Just pick them up from where they have fallen and pop them into your mouth. Enjoy it!)

Spreads

Here are a few delicious recipes for quick, healthful sandwich spreads that can make a honey of a meal. I always place at least one leaf of fresh lettuce on the bread with each of these spreads while making the sandwich. There is no reason why you couldn't add a few fresh vegetables sliced thin before you close the top on them, either.

HERB BUTTER

There isn't much to tell here. Herb butter is exactly what the title implies. Some butter with some herbs mixed into it. You have to have your butter soft, that is the only important thing. As for the herbs, use any combination that pleases you at the time. I always use chives and parsley to begin with, and then vary the others from time to time. Basil with a touch of garlic salt is good; tarragon and marjoram in even amounts, along with the parsley and chives, is also good. Use your own imagination.

½ cup butter, at room tem-   1 tablespoon rich cream
    perature   ½ cup herbs

Combine all the ingredients, blending until well mixed. Chill until ready to serve.

DATE-NUT SPREAD

ENOUGH FOR 3 SANDWICHES

1 fresh orange   1 cup walnuts
2 cups pitted dates   ¼ cup sesame or sunflower
¼ pound cream cheese, sof-   seeds (optional)
    tened to room temperature

Squeeze the orange, and set the juice aside. Cut off about one-quarter of the skin of the orange and put it into your blender with the dates. Whiz them around for a while until they are blended and then add the cream cheese, which is soft and has been sliced into small pieces. Whiz it again until the dates combine with the cheese and then add the orange juice and the nuts and whiz again. When everything is blended, remove from the blender and use what you need. It is nice sometimes to add about ¼ cup sesame or sunflower seeds here for added flavor. Refrigerate the remaining spread in a covered container.

AVOCADO SPREAD

ENOUGH FOR 2 SANDWICHES

Take one ripe (soft) avocado and peel it. Take out all the meat and place it in a bowl. Mash it up until it has a soft-butter consistency. Add a little salt and lemon juice and it is good enough. If you want something a little extra, you can add about 1 tablespoon of mayonnaise and 1 teaspoon of dry mustard. Some chopped cucumber added when you are mashing it up is yummy, too. Add a little chopped parsley with the mustard, it never hurts.

OLIVE SPREAD
ENOUGH FOR 3 SANDWICHES

1 *cup pitted olives*
¼ *pound cream cheese, softened to room temperature*

3 *green onions*
Salt (optional)
¼ *cup sunflower seeds*

Put the pitted olives in the blender and whiz them around until they are chopped up a bit. Chop up the onions by hand, and place them and the olives in a bowl and add the cream cheese. Mix everything around until they are all blended together. (You could add a little salt here, but I doubt if you will need it. Taste and see.) Now mix in the sunflower seeds and it is ready. Place on bread with a lettuce leaf and maybe even a slice of tomato or cucumber, and you will have a great sandwich.

Sandwiches are great for quick lunches, but I use them a lot at dinnertime when I have made a big pot of soup.

TAHINI SPREAD
ENOUGH FOR 4–5 SANDWICHES

1 *cup sesame seeds*
2 *tablespoons light vegetable oil*

¼ *cup light honey (more if you want, to your taste)*
Pinch of ground sea salt

Grind the seeds up in your blender. Add the oil to the honey and stir until they are blended. Put the seeds into a bowl, pour the honey mixture over them, and add the salt. Stir well, and there you are. Keep refrigerated when not using it, and be sure not to make too much.

TAHINI-PEANUT SPREAD

ENOUGH FOR 6 SANDWICHES

1 *cup sesame seeds*
2 *tablespoons sunflower seeds*
1 *cup peanut butter (preferably fresh home-made; page 28)*

⅓ *cup light honey*
3 *tablespoons light oil*
Pinch of salt *(optional)*

Grind the sesame and the sunflower seeds up in your blender. I assume that the peanut butter is already made, but, if it isn't, then make it now. Combine the honey with the oil and then pour it over the seeds. Mix well and add the peanut butter and the salt, if you need it. Mix well and taste. Not bad, huh?

Store in the refrigerator.

Dips

EGGPLANT AND OLIVE DIP

2–3 CUPS

1 *eggplant*
¼–½ *pound olives (I use black, and I chop them up a bit)*
1 *tablespoon grated onions or* 1 *teaspoon onion salt*

Juice of ½ *lemon*
Pinch of *pepper*
1 *pint sour cream*

Bake the eggplant at 350° for 1½ to 2 hours. Cool it and peel it. Chop it up in little pieces and blend it with the chopped olives.

Add the onion, lemon juice, pepper, and sour cream and chill about 1 hour. Serve it with some dandy home-make crackers, like Sesame Rounds (page 46).

COTTAGE-CHEESE DIP

ABOUT 3½ CUPS

This is a quick recipe that you can do in a few easy steps in your blender. Start with 1 pound of cottage cheese and add whatever you think will be nice for that day.

To start with, I grind up some sunflower seeds in the blender. Just a small handful is all that you will need. Now take the seeds out of the blender and put the cottage cheese in. Add some or all of the following to the cheese:

¼ teaspoon salt	*¼ onion, chopped fine*
¼ teaspoon celery salt	*Pinch of garlic salt*
Pinch of pepper	*Pinch of orégano*
1 teaspoon chives	*¼ cup blue cheese*
Pimento (enough to please you)	*¼ teaspoon horseradish*
	½ cup sour cream

Now, whiz it all up in the blender. You can add some fresh chopped vegetables now to the mixture and whiz it again, just for a few seconds, so that the vegetables are in small chunks, or you can set out small pieces of fresh-cut vegetables to dip into the dip. I use carrots, celery, cauliflower, mushrooms, and others, depending on the season of the year.

You can always change the recipe by adding and subtracting different ingredients. Say the cheese, for example. Instead of the blue cheese use some grated Cheddar and then add some anchovies and some basil and parsley instead of the orégano. If it ever seems to be a bit thin, then you can add a little arrowroot starch and mix it in well. Refrigerating for an hour or so will also help to firm it up a little.

SOUR-CREAM YOGURT DIP

ABOUT 1 QUART

1 pint sour cream
1 pint plain yogurt
¼ cup chopped chives

¼ cup diced green onions
1 teaspoon dry mustard
¼ teaspoon chili powder

Mix all the ingredients in a bowl and place it in the refrigerator to chill for about 2 hours.

Now comes the good part. Chop up a whole bunch of fresh vegetables like broccoli, cauliflower, carrots, zucchini, snow peas, cucumbers, radishes, and whatever else you see at the store that looks good. Now arrange the cut-up vegetables around the dip on a platter and serve. The vegetables dipped into the dip are wonderful, and, if most of the people haven't tried it before, I am sure that you will get lots of raves.

AVOCADO DIP

ABOUT 1 PINT

2 very ripe avocados
Juice of 1 lemon
¼ teaspoon chili powder or
   cayenne pepper

¼ teaspoon chopped parsley
Sunflower seeds

Remove the avocado meat from the skins and place in a bowl. Add the lemon juice, chili powder, and parsley and whip it with a wire whisk. When it is soft and mushy, add some sunflower seeds and it is ready to use as a dip for vegetables.

Cheese as an Appetizer

I am not one for serving appetizers, because I usually have so much to eat planned for a meal that there just wouldn't be any room for a pre-treat. However, if you feel that you have to serve something, one thing that I like to do is to put out a tray of varied soft cheeses with a knife and some crackers. I usually put out a chunk of:

Monterey Jack	*Swiss*
Mild Cheddar	*Brie*
Muenster	*Gruyère*
Camembert	

These are the ones that I use the most. The health food store where I shop carries goat's milk cheese, which I use sometimes if it is available. Put the cheeses that you select on a tray and serve them with a dish of fresh almonds. This should please your guests and not fill them up too much. One thing, I don't suggest that you use this for an appetizer if your main course contains cheese. Enough can be enough.

If you go to the health food store for your cheese, you will be amazed when you see that the Cheddar is the same color as the rest of the cheeses that they have. The processed cheese that you buy in the supermarket has lots of dyes in it that give it that orange color. The color certainly doesn't help the flavor, so why do you suppose they put it in? I have a theory: perhaps they put it in there to make it easier for us to find the cheese. How nice of them! Don't they think that we can read? Not to mention that after you have bought cheeses for a certain length of time (and it's not too long), it is easy to tell the different cheeses apart by their textures. By the way, while you are at the health food store looking at cheeses, why not pick up some goat's milk cheese and give it a try? It is a bit more expensive, but I think you might enjoy it.

Desserts

Fruit Desserts

WHIPPED CREAM WITH FRUIT

Do you know what real, honest-to-goodness home-made whipped cream tastes like? I do, and it is a real treat that is well worth trying. I always thought whipped cream only came from a can. It wasn't until I saw my girlfriend Arnelle whipping up some cream for a dessert one night that I knew how it was done. It's quite simple, too. All you need is:

1 *pint whole cream (Be sure that it is fresh)*	½ *teaspoon vanilla extract (Test for the vanilla, too, and add more if you want)*
2 *teaspoons honey (or more if you want; taste it as you whip it)*	

About an hour before you are going to whip the cream, put the bowl that you are going to use into the freezer of your refrigerator, along with the beaters from your hand mixer and the cream. Now, when you are ready, take them out and pour the cream into the bowl. If you don't have an electric hand mixer, you can do it with the kind with a handle on the side that you turn around—it will take a while longer. Anyway, put the cream into the bowl and start to whip it. Add the honey and the vanilla and keep whipping. In a few minutes you will see an amazing change. The cream will begin to thicken before your very eyes! As soon as it is thick enough for you, stop. Now you can use it as a topping on anything you want.

I suggest putting it over a bowl of any favorite fresh fruit of yours that happens to be in season. Slice the fruit in your favorite way and then just put a scoop of the cream on top. For a little extra flavor, sprinkle a touch of cinnamon or nutmeg on top.

For variety, you can use other flavorings, like peppermint or almond, instead of or along with the vanilla.

BAKED APPLES

4 SERVINGS

This is an old favorite of mine that I have boosted just a little from the way my mother used to put it together. I am giving you a recipe for 4 apples. You should always make one for every person, so if you need more make them.

4 *large green apples*
¼ *cup maple sugar or honey (The honey is better if you want the taste of the cinnamon to be dominant)*
1 ½ *tablespoons cinnamon*

½ *cup chopped walnuts or pecans*
¼ *cup butter*
1 *cup boiling spring water with* 1 *tablespoon honey in it*

Core the apples. Mix the sugar or honey with the cinnamon and most of the nuts. Put this into the cored apples and place the apples in a baking dish with a lid. Put 1 tablespoon butter on top of each apple and then pour the boiling water into the dish. Now sprinkle the extra nuts on top. Cover the dish and bake at 350°

for about 45 minutes, or until the apples begin to soften. Don't let them get too mushy.

CRUNCHY DESSERT

4–6 SERVINGS

8–10 *fresh apples, peaches, or pears, peeled and sliced*
¼ *cup light honey*
Pinch of salt

½ *teaspoon cinnamon*
¼ *cup chopped walnuts*
¼–½ *cup raisins (optional)*

Place the fruit in a flat 1½ quart casserole dish. (I use a 9-inch Pyrex baking dish.) Mix the honey with the salt and the cinnamon and pour the mixture over the fruit. Now sprinkle the chopped nuts and the raisins over the fruit.

Your next step is to make a topping out of the following ingredients:

2½ *cups raw oats (If you don't shop in a health food store where you can buy the oats in bulk, just measure out some of your Quaker Oats; they will be good enough)*
½ *cup whole-wheat pastry flour*

¼ *teaspoon salt*
⅓ *cup maple sugar or honey*
⅓ *cup light vegetable oil*
½ *cup chopped walnuts*
½–1 *teaspoon cinnamon (depending on your taste)*
½ *teaspoon vanilla extract*

When you finish the topping (I just squish all the ingredients together with my hands until the oil mixes evenly with everything else), sprinkle it all over the sliced fruit. Now bake the dish in a 375° oven for 40 minutes, or until the oats turn a nice brown. Remember, if you use a glass pan like I do, you should turn the oven down 25° no matter what you make. (The glass cooks faster, so you should use a lower temperature.) This is a delicious dessert, and it can be even better with a scoop of vanilla ice cream on top.

BANANA SURPRISE

4 SERVINGS

I like to call my dishes "surprise" because I am always telling my guests that I have a surprise for them in order to get them excited about the oncoming meal. It always works, and they always make me feel special after they have devoured their "surprise."

3 *ripe bananas*
¼ *cup light honey*
Juice of ½ *lemon*
1 *cup whipping cream*
  (*whole rich cream*)

1 *teaspoon vanilla extract*
Honey (*optional*)

Peel the bananas and put them in your blender. Whiz them around in the blender until they become soft and mushy. Add the honey and the lemon juice, and whiz them about again. Now put the mixture into a saucepan and cook it over a low flame until it reaches the boiling point. Remove it from the heat, place it in a bowl, and chill it in the refrigerator for 2 or 3 hours. Just before you are ready to take it out of the refrigerator, whip the cream with the vanilla extract and a little honey, if you want extra sweetness. When the cream is good and thick, fold the banana mixture into it. Serve it right away in little fruit cups or whatever you have around that it will look nice in.

You can make the same thing with strawberries, by substituting 1½ to 2 cups strawberries for the bananas and by adding 1 or 2 teaspoons arrowroot starch to the strawberries while they are cooking with the honey and the lemon juice.

Cakes

ALMOND CAKE

ABOUT 8 SERVINGS

2 cups sour cream
2 tablespoons yeast
½ cup warm water (not too hot, or you'll kill the yeast)
3 tablespoons honey
¼ cup softened butter
¼ teaspoon baking soda
2 teaspoons salt

2 eggs
6 cups sifted whole-wheat pastry flour
Almond paste
Chopped walnuts
¼ cup melted butter
Cinnamon

In a saucepan, heat the sour cream until it is lukewarm, not hot! In a large bowl mix the yeast with the warm water and then add the sour cream, honey, softened butter, baking soda, salt, and eggs. Mix well. Add one cup of the sifted flour and mix it in. Then add the rest of the flour and make a well-mixed dough. Turn the dough out onto a floured bread board and knead it. About 5 minutes will do. Place the dough in a well-greased bowl, cover it, and put it in a warm place to rise to about double its size.

When the dough has risen, divide it into 3 pieces and roll each one out to a square. Spread each square with almond paste and sprinkle some nuts on top of that. Now roll each square up like a jelly roll and cut into slices about 1 inch thick. Place the slices on a cookie sheet and let them rise again until they are doubled in size. Bake at 350° for 35 to 45 minutes. Remove them from the oven, spread with the melted butter, and sprinkle with cinnamon. Bake 10 minutes longer.

CARROT CAKE

ABOUT 10 SERVINGS

1 cup honey
4 eggs
1⅓ cups light vegetable oil
2 cups whole-wheat flour, sifted
2 teaspoons baking soda
2 teaspoons baking powder
2 teaspoons cinnamon
½ teaspoon of whatever spice you may like (I use ¼ tea-spoon nutmeg, and ¼ tea-spoon ginger; you could also just use allspice)
Chopped nuts (I use walnuts)
4 cups grated carrots
½ cup raisins (optional)

Sift dry ingredients together.

Beat the honey and eggs together with your hand mixer. Add the oil and beat for 2 minutes. Add the sifted dry ingredients and mix for 2 minutes more. Add 1 cup chopped nuts, the carrots, and the raisins. Pour into a greased 13 × 9½-inch loaf pan and bake at 350° for 40 minutes.

Spread the topping (see below) on the cake and sprinkle with a handful of chopped walnuts.

Chill about 2 hours, and what a treat!

TOPPING

½ pound cream cheese
Juice of ½ lemon

½ teaspoon vanilla extract

Beat the ingredients together with a hand mixer until they are soft and smooth.

FRUIT-FILLED CAKE

ABOUT 8 SERVINGS

Pick whatever fruit is in season, and cheap. Berries are always wonderful in the summer, apples in the fall. Peaches and nectarines are also good in this cake. Try mixing some peaches with a little blackberries or raspberries.

2 cups sifted whole-wheat pastry flour
1 teaspoon baking powder
½ teaspoon salt
½ cup light honey
½ cup butter, softened to room temperature

2 eggs
1 teaspoon vanilla extract
1 cup fresh fruit
Sprinkle of cinnamon (optional)
Chopped walnuts (optional)
Raisins (optional)

Sift the flour with the baking powder and the salt, then cream the honey with the butter. Beat in the eggs and the vanilla, and then add the flour and baking powder mixture and mix well until the batter is smooth and thick.

Pour half the dough into an ungreased baking dish and then spread the fruit over it. Sprinkle the fruit with a little cinnamon, if you want, and then place the rest of the dough around the fruit in clumps. Sprinkle the top with some chopped walnuts, if you want, also.

If you like raisins you could add some either with the fruit or sprinkle them on top with the nuts or by themselves.

Bake at 350° for 45 minutes.

MANDEL BREAD

ABOUT 4 DOZEN SLICES

½ cup butter
¾ cup honey
3 eggs
Juice from ½ orange or ½ lemon (I use both), plus rind
¼ teaspoon almond extract
2½–3 cups sifted whole-wheat pastry flour

2 teaspoons baking powder (Royal is the best brand)
½ teaspoon salt
½ teaspoon cinnamon
½ cup walnuts
¼ cup raisins (optional)
½ cup dates (optional)

Cream the butter and honey, then add the eggs and blend well. Add the juice and rind and almond extract. Sift the dry ingredients together and add to the batter, along with the nuts, raisins, and dates if you like them.

Form into 4 or 5 loaves or strips 2 to 3 inches wide, place on cookie sheets, and bake until golden brown (about 20 minutes at 400°). Cool slightly and slice. Return to the oven at 250° to dry for 10 minutes. (The older mandel bread is, within reason, the better it tastes. Bake it 2 days early, even though you'll probably eat it all while you're waiting the 2 days to serve it.)

This is great. The only thing missing from traditional mandel bread is the sprinkle of sugar for the top. But that's a simple sacrifice for good health. Besides, you could thin down some honey with a little lemon juice and brush it over the top before you put it into the oven to dry it.

POPPY-SEED CAKE

ABOUT 10 SERVINGS

¾ cup butter, softened to room temperature
¾ cup honey
2 eggs, separated
2 cups whole-wheat pastry flour
2 tablespoons baking powder
½ cup poppy seeds, soaked overnight
1 teaspoon almond extract
1 tablespoon spring water

Cream the butter with the honey and then beat about 2 minutes. Add the egg yolks and beat thoroughly. Mix in the drained poppy seeds. Sift the flour well, then sift in the baking powder. Add the poppy-seed mixture along with the almond extract and beat a few minutes. Beat the water into the egg whites until they are fluffy, then fold the egg whites into the batter.

Grease your baking pan and then line it with waxed paper. Now grease the paper, turn the batter into the pan, and bake at 350° for 45 minutes. (I don't know why you have to use the waxed paper—I guess it just helps when you want to get the cake out of the pan.)

SHARRON'S JIFFY COBBLER

4–6 SERVINGS

This recipe was given to me by my friend Sharron, who also is a *yenta*. She thinks vegetarianism is for the birds, but this recipe is a nice one for a quick dessert, so here it is.

6 tablespoons butter
1 cup sifted whole-wheat pastry flour
1 teaspoon baking powder
⅓ cup light honey

1 cup milk
2 cups fresh fruit (Blueberries, peaches, cherries, bananas, nectarines, and apples work well)

Decide on the pan you are going to use to bake the cobbler in. Sharron uses a 1-quart Corning Ware casserole dish, but I don't have any of those, so I use my Pyrex 1½-quart cake pan. (I am a real fan of Pyrex glassware. I use it as much as I can. One important thing to know about glass cooking dishes is that the oven should be turned down 25° from whatever the recipe calls for whenever you use them.)

Melt the butter in your baking dish over a low flame so that you don't brown it. When it is melted, add the flour, baking powder, honey, and milk. Mix them together and then pour the fruit on top. Bake at 350° for 45 minutes to 1 hour. (Note that I said 350°. For those of you who might use glass as I do, you should turn the oven down to 325°.)

STREUSEL COFFEE CAKE

ABOUT 8 SERVINGS

1½ cups plus 2 tablespoons sifted whole-wheat pastry flour
4 teaspoons baking powder
½ teaspoon salt
¼ cup plus 2 teaspoons butter
1 egg
⅓ cup light honey

½ cup milk
1 teaspoon vanilla extract
½ cup maple sugar (It's expensive, but it's good. You can use brown sugar if you want)
2 teaspoons cinnamon
½ cup chopped nuts

Sift together the 1½ cups flour, baking powder, and salt. Cut in the ¼ cup butter as though you were making a pie crust. Beat the egg together with the honey and then add them to the mixture, along with the milk and the vanilla, and beat the mixture well until it is blended.

Mix the sugar, the 2 tablespoons flour, cinnamon, and 2 teaspoons butter and blend well. Now add the nuts.

Pour half of the batter into a greased pan and sprinkle it with half of the sugar-cinnamon mixture. Add the remaining batter and the rest of the sugar-cinnamon mixture and then bake at 375° for 30 minutes.

Cookies

CHEWY OATMEAL COOKIES

4–5 DOZEN COOKIES

1 cup light vegetable oil
1 teaspoon lecithin
¾ cup honey

1 cup date or maple sugar
1½ teaspoons vanilla extract
1 teaspoon salt

1½ cups sifted whole-wheat   1 cup chopped nuts
   pastry flour   ½ cup raisins (optional)
¾ cup spring water   Sunflower seeds (optional)
5 cups rolled oats

Cream the oil, lecithin, honey, sugar, vanilla, and salt together. When they are nice and creamy, add the flour and the water and mix all the ingredients together until they are smooth. Add the oats, nuts and raisins (if you have to), and mix together well. Drop small spoonfuls onto a greased cookie sheet and press down on them with a fork. Bake at 350° for about 10 minutes, or until they begin to brown.

For a little change, add some sunflower seeds either with or instead of the nuts.

PEANUT-BUTTER TREATS

ABOUT 2 DOZEN COOKIES

½ cup peanut butter (Try   1 teaspoon vanilla extract
   making your own; page   ¼–½ cup raisins (optional)
   000)   1 cup sunflower seeds (op-
2 cups shredded coconut   tional)
¼ cup chopped walnuts
   (You can use something
   else)

Mix the peanut butter with half the coconut, nuts, raisins, and the vanilla. Take small globs and roll them into balls. Now roll each ball in the remaining coconut and put them on a greased cookie sheet. Place the cookie sheet in the refrigerator for about 2 hours, or until the cookies are firm.

If you want to double the recipe, use 1 cup of peanut butter, and leave the rest of the ingredients the same (or add 1 cup sunflower seeds to the mixture for more variety).

Pie

When I was growing up, I never had a piece of home-made pie. I have done a lot of reflecting on the subject, and I have decided that Jewish mothers don't bake fruit pies. If someone thinks that I am wrong, I would like to know it, but I can't ever remember seeing a home-made pie anywhere until I roomed with a girl from an old-fashioned Christian home who always baked pies. I also at the same time had a wonderful neighbor who used to bake pies all the time for her husband, to my utter amazement. I always thought that it was the hardest thing in the world to do, because I never saw it done.

Well, it took me a long time before I was brave enough to try it, but now I can't think of anything I enjoy serving more for dessert than a warm, home-made fruit pie. The only thing that I miss is the convenience of solid vegetable shortening. I had really got the crust down right with it when I had to stop using it because of the preservatives in it and change over to the oil method. The crust comes out good, but sometimes it can be a little touchy. One thing to remember is that when you use the oil method you will need considerably more flour than you do with a solid shortening.

MY PIE CRUST RECIPE
ENOUGH FOR A 10-INCH 2-CRUST PIE

3 cups sifted whole-wheat pastry flour, approximately
1 ¼ teaspoons salt
⅔ cup light vegetable oil

4–5 tablespoons cold water or milk (I usually use spring water)
¼ cup sesame seeds, approximately (optional)

Sift the flour with the salt. (I always do it at least two times.) Pour the oil into the water, but don't mix them, and then pour over the flour mixture in a bowl. Cut the ingredients together with a pastry cutter until a ball forms. If it seems to be a bit too oily, add a little more flour. Divide the dough into 2 balls. Flatten the first ball slightly and place between two pieces of waxed paper and roll it out as thin as you can on a bread board, if you have one (they certainly help). (I cover my board with two pieces of waxed paper and roll the dough out to the edges of the paper. This way I'm sure that I have a large enough crust, and it is usually the right thickness without too much effort.) For a little variety, add ¼ cup or less of sesame seeds to the flour and toss them in before you add the oil and the water mixture. Peel the top piece of paper off, and then carefully turn the dough into your pie pan, paper side up. Press the dough into the pan a little, and then remove the paper. If you are using a top crust or a lattice effect, roll out your other ball of dough the same way.

PEACH PIE

ABOUT 8 SERVINGS

You may want to use a little more honey than I do, because I use very little. I like to depend on the natural sweetness of the fruit, so I use as little honey as possible. Sometimes the fruit isn't too sweet and then I have a pretty tart pie, but I like tartness, and anyway I dig the suspense of not knowing just how the pie will taste until it is out of the oven. Use blackberries if they are in season. There certainly isn't anything wrong with a plain peach pie, but it is nice to have a little something extra to put in just before I get ready to fill the crust. If there just happens to be a few berries just hanging out in my refrigerator, well, the pie is as good a place for them as any.

¼ cup honey

Dash of salt

½ teaspoon cinnamon (more if you like)

4 tablespoons arrowroot starch

6 fresh peaches, peeled and sliced

½–1 cup blackberries

Pastry for a 10-inch 2-crust pie (page 159)

⅓ cup walnuts, approximately (optional)

2 tablespoons butter

Mix the honey, salt, cinnamon, and the starch until they are all blended together. Then pour the mixture over the sliced peaches and stir it all up. Add the berries, if you have some, or maybe some walnuts (about ⅓ cup) if you think that appeals to you. When the fruit is all coated with the honey mixture, put it into your pie crust shell and dot the butter on top. Place the top crust on it, or do whatever you want to do, but be sure to make some kind of hole-producing design on top of the pie so that the steam can come out while you are baking it. (My girl friend Ann has a little blue bird that she puts on top of her pies. He is hollow and he has a hole at his mouth where the steam escapes. It is so cute. Unfortunately I can't seem to find one any place to buy, so I have to make holes with a fork or knife.) If you use a lattice effect, then you already have steam-escape vents. Bake the pie in a hot oven, 400°, for 40 to 45 minutes, or until the crust is brown enough to suit you. Let it cool a little, but be sure to serve it warm. There is a difference between warm pie and cold pie.

I use this basic recipe for all my fruit and berry pies, so I think it is silly to spell out each one for you. Combination pies are more interesting than plain ones, and I'm sure that you can understand the reasoning behind that. Nectarines, pears, and apples, of course, are all good, as are cherries and most berries, except for strawberries because they get too soggy when you bake them and they don't taste as good. If you are into strawberries, use them in a yogurt pie that doesn't have to be baked.

PEACH-YOGURT PIE

ABOUT 8 SERVINGS

Make a single-shell pie crust in whatever method you find to be most satisfying. A graham-cracker crust would be good, I guess, but I prefer to use a regular crust (page 159) so that nothing takes away from the unique flavor of the filling. (Also, most of my pies are made in 10-inch glass pie pans, so if you use a smaller size you will have some filling left over. Why not eat it for lunch?) Bake the crust before you add the filling. (Remember to prick the bottom and sides well before baking so the pastry won't puff up, and to leave the oven heat 25° from the given temperature if you are baking in glass.) When it is the right color brown for you, then you know it is ready. Let it cool for about half an hour before you pour the filling into it.

FILLING

2 cups plain yogurt
¼ cup honey
2 teaspoons cinnamon
¼ teaspoon salt
¼ cup arrowroot starch

1 teaspoon vanilla extract
5 or 6 peaches, peeled and cut into slices
Sesame seeds (optional)

Put the yogurt in a bowl and add the honey, 2 teaspoons cinnamon, salt, starch, and vanilla. Mix it all together well and then stir in the fruit. Pour the mixture into the pie shell and sprinkle with a little more cinnamon on top. You could sprinkle a few sesame seeds on top, too.

This pie can be made with other fruit, too—just use your creative brain. I often add 1 cup of blueberries or blackberries whenever they are around, too. The pie is quite tart, but I sure like it.

YOGURT-CHEESE PIE

ABOUT 8 SERVINGS

CRUST

½ teaspoon vanilla extract
2 cups graham-cracker crumbs

¼ cup honey
¼ cup softened butter

Mix all the ingredients in a bowl. (I use my hand and sort of squish it until the ingredients are evenly distributed.) Then press it into a 10-inch glass pie pan and bake at 375° for 25 minutes.

FILLING

3 tablespoons arrowroot starch
Juice of ½ lemon or ½ orange

¼ cup honey
¾ teaspoon vanilla extract
1 pound cream cheese
2 cups yogurt

Stir the starch, juice, honey, and vanilla in a cup to a smooth pasty texture. Then blend together with the cream cheese till smooth. Add the yogurt and beat 2 minutes with a hand mixer. Pour into the cooled crust and refrigerate at least 10 hours. The longer the better. Why not try for 24?

This makes Sara Lee look like a machine.

Carob Desserts

Carob is a chocolate substitute, which when it is used well can be almost as delicious and not nearly as fattening for you. Chocolate has a fat content of 52 percent as compared to carob, which has a fat content of only 2 percent.

I buy carob in the health food store in powder form, just like cocoa comes in the supermarket. I found that it took a while to get used to, and I must admit that I still do sneak out for chocolate every once in a while. The only problem with that is that the chocolate always has sugar in it instead of honey, so it is less and less often that I do go for the chocolate. Give carob a try and see what dandies you can make up with it.

Carob doesn't work quite the same as cocoa or chocolate, so here is a simple conversion that can help you change any recipe that calls for chocolate or cocoa.

3 tablespoons carob powder + 2 tablespoons spring water = 1 ounce chocolate
1 ounce chocolate = 1 square

CAROB PUDDING

4–6 SERVINGS

1 *quart milk*
½ *cup light honey*
1 *teaspoon Pero (This is a coffee substitute, which I buy in the health food store, that has no caffeine in it. If you want to use instant coffee, go ahead; I wouldn't, though)*

½ *teaspoon salt*
¼ *cup carob powder*
1 *teaspoon vanilla extract*
6 *tablespoons arrowroot starch*
¼ *cup shredded coconut*
½ *cup chopped walnuts*
¼ *cup mixed sesame and sunflower seeds*

Heat the milk in your double boiler over a medium flame. Add the honey, Pero, salt, carob, and vanilla, stirring constantly as you add them. Now add the arrowroot starch, stirring constantly until the pudding begins to thicken. When it begins to thicken, stir in the coconut, nuts, and seeds and keep stirring. When the pudding is thick enough, remove from the heat and pour it into dessert cups. (I don't have dessert cups, so I use ceramic mugs that I usually use for serving tea. I like the way it looks in them, and they certainly do the job, so I see no reason to get dessert cups.)

CAROB TOPPING

MAKES ABOUT 2 CUPS

1⅛ cups carob powder
¾ cup spring water
½ cup sour cream
Pinch of salt
½ teaspoon cinnamon (optional)

¼ cup cream
1 teaspoon arrowroot starch
Honey (optional)

Mix the carob powder and water in a double boiler. Blend in the remaining ingredients except the honey and heat over a low flame until the ingredients are smooth and as thick as desired. Test for sweetness, and add a little honey if you want it. (If you add more than 2 teaspoons of honey, you may need a little more arrowroot for thickness again.) Serve this topping over ice cream or cake.

CAROB CANDY

ABOUT ½ POUND

This is the recipe that I suggest you use first when you are about to discover carob for the first time. Everyone I serve this to loves it, and they say they can't tell it isn't chocolate.

½ cup coconut oil

½ cup honey

3 tablespoons powdered soy milk

1 tablespoon arrowroot starch

3 tablespoons carob

1 teaspoon vanilla extract

1½ cups chopped walnuts

½ cup sunflower seeds

½ cup shredded coconut

Melt the coconut oil until you have ½ cup. (Coconut oil comes in a jar in solid form, so all you have to do is unscrew the lid and put the jar in a pan of boiling water for a few minutes until enough melts. There is no reason to wait for it all to melt, just what you need. When you have what you need, remove the jar from the water, wipe it off and then put it into the refrigerator.) Mix the coconut oil with the honey, soy milk, arrowroot, carob, and vanilla, until they are well combined. Add the nuts, seeds, and coconut and mix it up well. Pour the mixture into a shallow pan and chill in the refrigerator for 2 to 3 hours. When it is firm, cut it into bars and serve it. (Don't serve more than you need, because it will begin to soften if left out at room temperature for a long period of time.)

Beverages

COCONUT MILK

ABOUT 2 CUPS

2 *cups spring water*
2 *cups shredded coconut*

1 ½ *teaspoons honey*
Pinch of salt

Bring the water to a boil. After it has boiled a few minutes, pour it over the coconut shreds, which you have placed in the blender. Let it sit for a few minutes, then run the blender until a milky liquid forms. Add the honey and the salt and run the blender again for a few seconds. When it looks like milk, strain it and then refrigerate it for a few hours in a covered container. It is good just as it is, or else it makes a nice base for any drink (one follows) that calls for milk.

FRESH TOMATO JUICE

ABOUT 2 QUARTS

10 *very ripe tomatoes*
2 *green onions*
Juice of 1 *lemon*

Salt to taste
¼ *cup sunflower seeds*

Cut up the tomatoes into little pieces and put them into your blender. Do the same with the onions. Now liquefy them in the blender. When they are in liquid form, pour into a saucepan and cook for about half an hour, stirring frequently.

Squeeze the lemon and add the juice to the mixture, along with a little salt. Grind up the sunflower seeds in your blender and set them aside. Strain the juice a couple of times and then add the ground-up seeds. Chill in the refrigerator for at least 5 hours in a covered container and then serve.

Allow everyone the choice of salt to taste and serve extra lemon pieces in case anyone likes his tomato juice supertart, like I do.

FRESH CRANBERRY JUICE

ABOUT 1½ QUARTS

Cranberry juice is one of nature's healers. It is very good for helping to cure a urinary infection, because it has a way of flushing out the bladder. It is thus a good juice to drink all the time, for it helps to keep your bladder in good working condition. The only problem is that cranberries are only in season in the fall and early winter months. As I happen to prefer fresh juice to bottled, I drink a lot of it from October to January and hope that it has a lingering effect. It is good though, so make it when it is available.

1 *pound cranberries*   *Honey to taste*
1 *quart spring water*

Using a pan with a cover, cook the cranberries in the water until they are soft; it shouldn't take more than half an hour. When they are soft, place them with the water in your blender and whiz them around until they liquefy. (Don't do more than 1½ cups at a time, because the mixture will increase in volume

as you work the blender, and if you put more in it will overflow.)
When all the cranberries have been liquefied, put the juice through
a strainer. (This step is optional.) Now place the juice in a
container with a lid and put it into your refrigerator to chill.
Serve it with or without ice cubes, depending on how cold
you let it get.

LEMONADE

1 QUART PLUS

6 *lemons*
1 *quart spring water*
¼ *cup honey (light honey is
definitely preferred here)*

*Fresh mint (if you have
some)*

Squeeze the juice from the lemons, and pour it into the spring
water.

Clean out two of the lemons and add the pulp if you want to.
It makes it stronger, and I like it that way. Now stir in the honey
and pour the mixture over tall glasses full of ice cubes made
from spring water. Add a few fresh mint leaves and you're all
set for a cool refresher.

I recommend that you use light honey here so that the flavor
isn't noticeable. Wildflower is the one that I use the most when
I don't want to have a noticeable honey flavor. You should test
the lemonade for sweetness, when you stir it into the mixture.
You may want to use more than I do. I like things tart.

LEMON-GRAPE ADE

1 QUART PLUS

6 *lemons*
2 *cups Concord grapes, approximately*

1 *quart spring water*
¼ *cup honey*

Squeeze the lemons, and then put the grapes into your blender and whiz them around for a while. (I usually take the seeds out before I put the grapes in the blender, but I don't think that it makes that much difference.) After you whiz the grapes and they liquefy, strain them a couple of times through a small strainer. (It may be easier to mix the grapes with a cup of the spring water first and then strain it. The mixture will be thinner then and thus go through a lot easier.) Take some of the pulp from two of the lemons and add it with the lemon juice and the grape juice to the rest of the water. Mix in the honey and then taste it for sweetness. Fix it up to suit your taste, and then pour it over some ice cubes made from spring water.

FRUIT SURPRISE

ABOUT 2½ CUPS

2 cups fresh fruit juice (Use pineapple if it is in season)

2 cups fresh berries (You can use any fruit that you want, as long as it complements the juice that you are using in the drink. Your taste buds are the judge)

1 banana

2 teaspoons shredded coconut (optional, but do give it a try)

Honey (if you want—no more than a teaspoon if any, I would guess)

Take your juice, which you have probably had to squeeze yourself (if you are using pineapple, all you have to do is cut up chunks, put them into the blender, and liquefy them. Then strain the remaining pulp and you have the juice), and put it into the blender along with the fruit. Whiz it up until the fruit is dissolved and then taste it. If you want to add honey, do it now and then run the blender again for a quick go. Pour the drink into glasses, float a few pieces of whole fruit on top, and serve.

FRUIT SHAKES

ABOUT 2½ CUPS

1 *cup fresh fruit*
1 *cup milk (Try using soy milk)*

1 *cup vanilla ice cream*
1 *teaspoon honey (optional)*
1 *banana (optional)*

Clean the fruit and peel it if it has to be peeled. Cut it into little pieces and put it into your blender. Add the milk, the ice cream, and the honey, if you want it. (I rarely use the honey because I like to rely on the natural sweetness of the fruit. If I use a banana along with the cup of fresh fruit I never use the honey, and I recommend that you leave it out, too.) Now whiz the ingredients in the blender until they are combined. Don't let it go too long or it will get thin. The thicker the better, don't you agree? Serve it right away, nice and cool.

FRUIT SMOOTHIE

ABOUT 2½ CUPS

1 *banana*
½ *peach (in season)*
½ *pear (in season)*
6 *strawberries (in season)*
1 *cup fresh orange juice (or*

whatever your favorite flavor may be)
1 *teaspoon honey*
¼ *cup yogurt*

Place all of the above ingredients in your blender and whiz around for a few seconds. Pour it into glasses and wow, what a surprise there is in store for you!

Now, if you really want to do something good for yourself, put about 2 tablespoons of wheat germ or wheat-germ oil in it before you whiz it in the blender, and you have an enjoyable "health drink."

This drink can have countless combinations. Just trust yourself and see what you can think up.

Index

Maureen Goldsmith

Maureen Goldsmith (born 1946, Pisces) grew up in Chicago, and after much travel through Europe, the States, and various educational institutions, discovered San Francisco and made it her home. She pots well enough to please herself, sews with sufficient skill to make a living at it, and is the soul and sole impresario of a private eating club, famous on the West Coast, called—what else?—The Organic Yenta.